THRIVING
WITH OUR SCARS:

12 Steps Towards
Complete Restoration

By **Regina Clay**

For more information on book purchasing or promotional use, please contact ceo@reginaclay.com.

Edits and layout: solfire@phoenix-farm.com
All Photos by Andre Dunston of Epic Media Photography

ISBN: 9781691513499
FIRST EDITION

DEDICATION

I dedicate this book first and foremost to miracle #1 Alisa and miracle #2 Antonio. They have been with me during most of this journey and I am grateful for them both.

I also dedicate this book to my parents who at the time of publishing are both still living: Jasper and Ossie Clay and to my brother Reginald.

Family is everything to me.

TABLE OF CONTENTS

FORWARD

Congratulations on starting a journey that I am sure will be one that you will always remember. I believe that we all have a mandate to THRIVE! Thriving is a much different mindset, attitude and way of living than Surviving. So many times we are advised to "make it through" our challenges, adversity, hardships, calamities and misfortunes in life and business — however making it through is for victims. You are not that. You are victorious. You are a winner. You are a champion. You are a Thriver! Because of all of that...my friend, you are necessary! And that is exactly what Regina M. Clay wants you to fully know, understand and internalize through this book.

Scars are something that we all have in common. Scars are something that we can't get dressed or undressed without seeing. Scars come in all shapes, sizes, colors, textures and forms. They come in all types of people, places, things, events and experiences. Scars are the proof of the Healing Power of God and the Resilient Power of the Human Spirit. Scars are the proof that we survived. We made it. We are still here. Every one of us has scars...and since all scars are proof of injury, there is no point in judging whose scar is better or worse than another. Through this amazing book, Regina M. Clay challenges us all to learn how to Thrive With Our Scars. Through the stories, examples, ideas, insights, inspiration and transparency that you will surely see in this book, Regina's goal is to get you to view the scars in your life differently and see them as stepping stones to your greatest levels of success ever.

I challenge you to not only read this book but really take it in!

Really ingest the content from a new vantage point. Highlight, dog-ear, share some powerful thoughts and quotes on social media and tell others about the powerful breakthroughs that you are getting from this eloquent book. I've had the great privilege of knowing Regina M. Clay for over 6 years. During that time, I've watched with my own eyes as Regina has done the very thing she is challenging you to do in this book. I've watched her be an amazing mother to her 2 children, a wonderful daughter to her loving parents, a devoted sister to her siblings, a pastor, preacher, teacher, speaker, influencer, community leader, mentor, coach, connector, networker, virtual COO and entrepreneur. I've watched her carry each of these titles all while having to Thrive with her own challenges and adversities and still come out on top.

So you're learning from someone who hasn't just read something cute in a book — she's LIVED what she is sharing and she's helped countless others to learn these principles as well.

Now it's your turn! Are you ready to stop blaming, stop complaining, stop throwing a pity party, and start Thriving With Your Scars?

If so, then allow me to introduce to some and present to others . . . my amazing friend and Big Sister . . . *Regina M. Clay.*

Thriving with You,

Delatorro L. McNeal, II MS, CSP

Chairman & CEO of Platinum Performance Global, LLC
Global Peak Performance Expert & Speaker, Best Selling 7x
Author, Television Personality

INTRODUCTION

She walked into a room and all they did was stare. Some looked on in jealousy. Some looked on in judgment. Some looked on in admiration. Some looked in anticipation. But the unfortunate truth was that as many as there were that looked at her, they still couldn't see her.

No, no one had any genuine idea of who she was.

A woman, a daughter, a sister, and mother. A college graduate, an entrepreneur, a public figure, a political activist, a coach, a female pastor, a sister in two national organizations. All of these titles are admirable and each one has its own dynamics. In fact, you can picture a specific type of person with each title. But what if those titles held *other* titles within them – ones that weren't so welcomed and desired?

Can you picture any of the previously mentioned titles, coupled with ones like ex-wife or ex-inmate? And what about ex-addict? Yes, these titles once accompanied the others – some did so simultaneously!

She is I and I am she. My name is Regina Clay and I have embodied each and every one of those titles, among others, at some time or another. What's even crazier is that I was able to hide some of the *not so pretty titles*. Yes, there was a time when most who thought they knew me had NO idea what I was going through nor the detriment that I was facing. Throughout my lifetime there have been and will be many who'll see me and have no idea of what it takes to be me. Some will envy the outer appearance or the prestige they think I have. Some will whisper about the connections I have, wondering how and why I became so *lucky*. But let me tell you right now: *I'm not lucky. I'm loved! I'm not lucky. I'm blessed! I'm not lucky; I'm simply thriving with my scars!*

By definition, a *scar* is a mark left by a "healed" wound! (Please catch that, because it's important!!!) It's also defined as any blemish remaining as a trace of injury. So to make it plainer, a scar is merely a reminder that you've survived something. It's indicative of your ability to endure. It solidifies the fact that you have lived through something that could have potentially killed you.

Even when a scar is unattractive, even when it tells a story that you may want hidden, even if it serves as a reminder of the bad – know that it's symbolic of the good. And the good thing about it is this: you're living, you're thriving, and you're making moves that you once deemed impossible. But let's be honest, that can be uncomfortable at times.

Scars look differently, are shaped differently, and occur for different reasons. Did you know that some scars aren't visible? Yes, we know what a scar looks like on the surface of our skin. We can tell when someone has had surgery or experienced a burn. A mark on the skin will indicate a cut or even major surgery. But what about those internal scars? What about the scars that nobody can see, yet are still felt? What about the scars from words and emotions that have left a mark larger than can be described? Yes, those scars also exist. Some of them still hurt decades after their creation.

If I were to tell you about each and every scar that I've ever had, we'd run out of time. And if I told you stories about the scars that I've inflicted, you'd be surprised. The truth is that every one of us are scarred. We all have had things to happen to us that have left a mark. Most of the time we only cause more distress to ourselves by pretending those scars (or the events surrounding them) don't and didn't exist. We then inflict more pressure on ourselves to keep up these illusions. But there comes a time when we have to acknowledge the scar and be ok with its existence. That doesn't mean we live life through a scarred vision; however, we should live our vision through and beyond our scars. And that is what this book is all about!

My desire is to help you know that living and thriving *with* your scars is possible.

Oftentimes, we're made to think that our scars should cripple us or deter us from walking out into the life we dream of claiming for ourselves. Many of us even use our scars, or the circumstances that caused them, as a reason to be stagnant and unproductive.

Now is the time to experience something different. Now is the time to recognize that what happened to you is *not* the end of you! If anything, it's merely fuel to propel you where you need to be. So in order for you to think and feel in a new way, you have to go back to your genesis – to your beginning. We often miss out on the lesson behind some of life's pains and tests due to not wanting to relive certain things. But it's necessary, especially if we want to truly thrive and live the life we were created to live!

Going back to the beginning can take a toll on your mental and emotional states. Doing that forces us to relive moments that made us sad, made us feel ashamed, made us angry, and a plethora of other sentiments. While not all memories are horrific, it's usually the bad ones that stick out. It's funny how life can make us remember the ugly much quicker than the beautiful. But for that reason, we live our lives through lies.

In order to fight back against the natural mental tendency to focus on the negative memories, many of us spend time pretending that none of these negatives ever happened. We put on our masks, hoping that no one sees what really lies beneath. We smile when prompted and laugh on demand, as long as it means our truths are hidden. Instead we must realize that our unwillingness to *look back* doesn't change anything. In order to overcome the past, we have to accept reality. We have to embrace the unpleasantness of such things that come up in our minds. And in doing that, we have to acknowledge that we *do* have scars. But guess what? Our scars are beautiful! We can begin to see them as such!

This book will give you steps that I used myself, in no specific order, to push myself to greater! I come from a very strong family and my parents are known as pillars in our community. And while they've not shunned me because of my scars, the thoughts I used to think of myself caused *me* to treat *me* differently. I stopped fully believing in love and peace. I searched for the right things, but in the wrong places. I've always had a heart which wanted to serve, but not even serving others could help me when I was struggling with overwhelming negative self-thinking. I have the capacity to show compassion, but not even that could save me from my issues. I had to take a look in the mirror and make a conscious decision to do things differently. I had to allow God to reorder my steps. Most astoundingly and hardest of all, I had to stop getting in His way. I had to acknowledge all of my truths, not just the portions I wanted to accept.

ALL of it had to be embraced.

Why? Because ALL of it made me *ME*! And for that reason, I'm now at a place of healing and restoration. I am in a place where I can share a few things that I had to implement to get me here. And finally, I know I can help you thrive with your scars. Because thriving *is* possible and restoration *is* available. You just have to know how to use the scars as fuel and not look at them as failures.

Come with me, if you will, on a journey. At the end of these 12 Steps you will be prepared to do what you've been afraid to do all along – LIVE!

So now, let's begin to live…

Regina Clay

CHAPTER ONE

DECISIONS, DECISIONS

MAKING UP YOUR MIND ABOUT YOUR GROWTH

Life is about decisions! We're always contemplating what to wear or what to eat, what to listen to or what movie to watch. We make decisions about which route to take to work or to the store, and we make decisions on whether or not to respond to those text messages. We even decide whether or not we should post "that" on social media. But one of the decisions we rarely make is the one that causes us to look at where we are, and decide to be better!

Being *better* and not *bitter* is all a matter of choosing. We can't often comprehend that, neither can we embrace that type of power – because we've usually become comfortable where we are. And the sad thing is — while we think we're comfortable in that place, our destiny and purpose are screaming for a way to get out of that rut and manifest.

It's synonymous with a 10 year old still trying to wear clothing made for 3-6 month olds. Unless there is a medical condition involved, you'll most likely not see such a thing. And that's because it's preposterous to think that a whole walking and talking human being, maybe the size of a small adult, can fit into something that tiny. Humans were meant to grow! Even as adults, we know when a pair of pants or shoes no longer fit us; yet when we force them to, we end up in more pain or almost injuring ourselves. There has to come a time when you honestly recognize that *it* just doesn't fit anymore . . . All of this starts with what? *A decision!*

While we make decisions everyday about everything, even when we're not trying to, we often fail at making decisions that will produce and promote wealth, success, health, elevation, or any type of positive growth. We need to ask ourselves this question: *Why don't I feel like I'm worthy of having those things?*

Somewhere along the line you made up your mind about yourself. Unfortunately for most of us, it wasn't the best vision of ourselves that we settled on. You decided that all the negative things that occurred and all the mistakes you made disqualified you from being better than your past. You decided that a failed marriage or a miscarriage meant you were no longer loveable. You decided the addictions or the criminal record snatched you out of the running for the next blessing. My, oh my, were you wrong!

You see, it's those exact things that put you in a position to be and accept favorable. How else will you receive *and* appreciate a blessing if you never endured the storms? In the natural world a rainbow only shows up *after* some rain or after a heavy storm. Doesn't it appear that their existence is dependent upon each other? Just like your good days and bad days. But even while in the storm, a decision has to be made:

- Do I grab the umbrella or stay inside?
- Do I run off the porch and embrace the rain?
- Do I sit and look out of the window?

The reality is that no matter what you do, the rain will still fall.

Therefore it's helping someone or something that is the decision that can make a change for the better. So why not embrace it? Why not see where it takes you? See what type of beautiful rainbow your new behavior will create at the end of this storm you are in right now. Do you even believe a rainbow will come?

That appears to be the real question. However, if we read and believe biblical scriptures, we know that this is a guarantee. For example, what about Romans 8:28 which states, "And we know that all things work together for good to them that love God, to them who are the called according to His purpose." This means that every ounce of weather, every chaotic occurrence, every bit of heartache – it all was predestined to work for our good. Yet and still, we were tricked into deciding that these challenges weren't beneficial. That is far from the truth.

Unfortunately, we focus so much on the storm and on the winds and on the lightning and thunder, that we negate what's going on through the process of living through the storm. We can't even fathom that it's producing something in us, through us, or for us that will catapult us to a better place. So with the rain, we don't realize that it had to come down hard so that something could be watered. We don't consider that maybe there was an area in drought in our souls that needed the moisture. We simply don't like rain because someone made us believe that it was bad, that it was a time to fear, that it was indicative of disaster. To the contrary, every bit of rain that falls has a purpose. And every bit of aggravation and testing that you have experienced in your life *all* had purpose. Once you can accept this, you have begun the process toward making the decision that you deserve to grow and succeed.

Making up your mind about your growth, and believing that you deserve to grow, can lead you on a path of peace that you never imagined. But before you make the actual decision to grow, you have to first not be afraid to simply *think* about your growth. Believe that it's possible, understand that it's necessary, visualize that it's already yours. Being able to do this usually means you have to forgive yourself.

You've got to forgive yourself for the bad decisions you made, whether you knew better or not. You have to be willing to acknowledge that you did mess up, but that mess up is not the foundation of who you are. You have to know, without a shadow of a doubt, that you're not your past and you don't get to judge yourself by your past. Every single thought that you have about yourself starts with a decision to think better of yourself. It goes beyond that. For me, I had to forgive myself for choosing an abortion and for losing the ability to love who I was raised and called to be.

During my college years, one of the most devastating occurrences for me was when I made the decision to terminate my pregnancy. I wasn't alone in making that decision; the father was in agreement and with me during the process. While it seemed easy to do, the aftermath of that decision played with my emotions and my psyche more than I was prepared for. I was in college and doing very well for myself. I was intelligent and well known in my community and on campus. People loved and respected me, especially in the church. But – there I was, a church girl, having sex before marriage. Everything I was taught and knew to be true seemed to be put on the back burner during that time of my life. Before I knew it, my decision to have the abortion led to another decision – getting high to escape the mental pain.

I also was escaping the misleading bond with a man I thought would never disappear from my life. Then came the downward spiral. One bad decision after another, one lie being believed after another, one ounce of morality dying after another. Yes, that was my reality. That was my life. And soon after this downward spiral started, it led to my suspension from college.

As you can see, decisions play a vital role in everything we do and everything we are. In the midst of our decision-making we have to be real and honest about who we are and who or what we're connected to if we really want to make the best decisions possible. Once we have that reality check with ourselves, we just might find out that we need to make some changes. Most of the time, the changes are forcing themselves to be made anyway; we just refuse to acknowledge it which pushes the inevitable down the line a little further. Why? Because dysfunction can become comfortable and attractive.

You have to let go of toxic relationships, even the ones that seemingly feel good to you! You'd be surprised how much energy you can waste on a person. Trust me, I know. I remember giving energy and time to the wrong people -- from college up through my young adulthood. I even remember a time when I was giving the wrong energy to myself. (*Yes, it's possible to have a toxic relationship with YOU!*)

I allowed myself to participate in things that weren't beneficial to my growth toward who I wanted to be. I fell into sync with addictions. Addictions became my significant other and I was faithful to it; unfortunately, it wasn't faithful to me. And what happens in one-sided relationships? Someone has to lose! Someone gets hurt! Someone ends up in a place they don't want to be! And it never ends well – until you decide to do something different and be something different! (*Oh my, there goes that word again – DECISIONS!*)

Of all the definitions of restoration and all the words with similar meanings, I've found that renewal and revival stick out the most to me. They indicate that something or someone has another chance. The prefix "re" means "again," which indicates that it has once been done and has the opportunity to emerge once more. If you want restoration, why not re-decide? Why not re-believe? Why not re-consider? Why not re-try? No matter how far down or around you have gone, the possibility to turn and get to a path you really want to be on is available. You just have to decide if you're strong enough for the turn. And I'm pretty sure that you are!

Decide that you want to reconnect with your purpose and rebuild the right kind of relationships that are meaningful to your growth. Decide that you will no longer be held hostage by the mistakes that you've made. Decide that healing is yours and that the right type of growth will be your new normal. Decide that your next steps are indicative of your future, not your past! YOU decide!

There's a scripture that says, "Choose ye this day whom ye will serve." Today, I want you to choose which version of you that you will serve! Will you continue to let the past be your puppet master? Or will you press forward and let the destiny that you deserve set you up for the life you're called to have?

At the end of the day, the choice is yours! Make sure you choose wisely. Change your thoughts by changing your speech and your surroundings – it all takes a little action. Behave your way into a new normal. Remember this principle: *If it doesn't add to you, it's subtracting from you!*

Don't allow negativity to turn you into a decreasing mathematical problem. You're more than that! You just have to decide that you are!

Here is an affirmation that you can declare over yourself about making decisions to grow:

My thoughts have the power to change my outcome.

My outcome has the power to change nations.

And with this power, I will decide what's best for me – at all times. I will decide that I'm worth investing in my peace and joy and maturity. I will decide that no decision is too difficult for me to make, especially when it points me in a direction of healing and wholeness.

My mind is not confused. My mind is not clouded. My mind is not under attack. I am at peace and I will use my power to embrace the elevation that is longing for me, as I long for it.

CHAPTER TWO

WALK IN YOUR TRUTH

EMBRACING EVERY PART OF YOUR JOURNEY

One of the most aggravating things to hear is someone denying that you've been through *all* that you've been through – especially when they haven't a clue!!!

The saying is that we should never judge a book by its cover; yet, there are those who will look at the cover, look at the title, and automatically assume that our bad days and trials weren't as deep as we know they were. Some find it hard to believe that we genuinely don't look like what we've been through. The harsh reality is that some people would much rather us look like all the pain and suffering and detriment that we've experienced *and* caused in our life. They want to see all of our past on our faces out of morbid curiosity. But God is gracious! He keeps us covered, even when we don't deserve it.

"There's no way she's ever done that!" Yeah, I'm sure that's what most people think when they read any ounce of my personal story. Whether I'm standing before an audience of thousands or looking one person in the eyes, people see my "after" but don't understand my "before" at all.

Yes, I had a very good childhood. My parents were well known in their community and respected. My family was supportive and my brother and I knew what it was to be loved. But the truth is that I was always looking for something more. The truth is that I made some bad choices and I made some decisions that I didn't know would hurt me later in life the way they did. The truth is that I had to learn to love and accept myself – and that's still something I have to do daily. But if you were to meet me for the first time or hear me speak, you would never believe that I once battled with addictions or low self-esteem. You would never know that I looked for love in the wrong places, that I settled for less when I shouldn't have. The reality is that I did all those things – notice that's *past tense*. Yes, *I did*! I did those things, but those things are not who I am. And it took me being able to accept and walk in my truth to be able to share with you how you can do this, too!

If you truly want to walk in your truth and embrace *all* of your past, no matter what took place, you have to first recognize this: there's absolutely NOTHING wrong with caring about YOU!

Often times, leeches come in the form of people who will suck the life and growth out of you. They'll try to diminish and minimize your story. They'll even try to find ways to edit it in their minds, and discredit your push to live life abundantly. You have to stay away from such people. These people will always create their version of your reality and expect you to latch onto that vision they push forth. That is NOT proper!

It's like listening to a famous song that's been around for years, knowing the lyrics, and meeting someone who says, "Well it would sound better this way!" *How rude*!

The point is that reality is reality, regardless of who accepts it or not. And your truth, your story, is just that – no matter who disapproves of it or sees other things in your past or your chances at different futures. You have to ask yourself this question: *Why don't I feel good about my truth*?

While nobody can tell your story like you can, there are times when you don't like it or don't want to share it because there's a part of you that's still ashamed of it. There are elements of you that have been made to feel ashamed and horrible for so long that you've taken "their" opinions as your own. What does this indicate? It shows that you've not exercised honesty in your own life with and about your own self. That can be dangerous. Because if you can't be honest with yourself, you'll never really be honest with anyone else.

One of the things we have to teach ourselves is that each and every part of our journey was and is necessary. The heat, the eating, the breaking, the separation – it was all needed to pull something out of you. Even when it doesn't seem like it's working for your good, it is. According to Romans 8:28, *ALL* things actually work for our good. That means even the stuff that we hate about our past. That includes the secret encounters we've had and the inappropriateness we had to endure. As tough as it is, and as much as it might still bother you, I want you to be free from the shame and guilt that try to associate themselves with your story. Because you wouldn't be *you* if it had not been for all that you've seen and suffered. Once again, you have to make up in your mind that YOU will be the first one to accept your life, your story, and all of the chapters that have been written so far. Only then can you embrace the amazing future that's waiting to welcome you with open arms.

In order to get to this level of boldness, you have to consider the 3 levels of you that you have to love and appreciate:

Who you were,
Who you are, and
Who you're becoming.

You can't accept one without the other. You can't share one without the other. That is the trinity of your reality just as God (the Father, the Son, & the Holy Ghost) is the Trinity for your existence.

Once you've embraced those levels, you simply live out loud! Realize it's not about bragging on self; it's more about bragging on the grace and mercy that has been extended to you in all walks of your life.

It's about recognizing that you are truly blessed and favored. It's about knowing and accepting that your trials were meant to make you triumphant and your tests were created for powerful testimonies. Again, this can only happen when you decide to embrace your journey. Even a Thanksgiving meal has to endure a specific process for successful preparation. Even diamonds and metals have to go through fire in order to be made pure and strong. And just to prove the necessity of such trials, the following scripture says it clearly: *But He knoweth the way that I take: when He hath tried me, I shall come forth as gold.* This is found in Job 23:10 and gives us a hint at a "before and after" process. First, one must be tried. Second, they'll come forth as gold. And the gold embraces its truth – the truth that it had to endure something uncomfortable to become comfortable.

In case you need another example, let's look at 1st Peter 5:10, that says, "…after that ye have suffered a while, make you perfect, stablish, strengthen, settle you." So once again, there's a *before* and there's an *after*. But the *before* must come if you want to reap the benefits of the *after*. This only occurs and begins to make sense when you can see and appreciate both sides.

Most of you reading this may be struggling with accepting and embracing your journey. The truth is that some of the things you faced were NOT your fault! You might have even made this statement: *I didn't ask to be here!* What's so beautiful about this life is that you're needed. While you didn't ask for it and while you may have even wanted to end this journey, your presence is an enhancement to the earth. Didn't you know that?

Yes, every ounce of betrayal, every rejection, every mistake, every unfair occurrence – it was all necessary for you to be here, to be alive, and to make this world better. You have a gift that only you can bring to the table. You have a story that only you can share to the masses. You have wisdom that can only be received by you in certain audiences.

Until you embrace your journey and know that YOUR truth is the greatest love story of all, nothing else will matter. So your challenge is to not be afraid of thinking about the past. Don't be afraid of remembering what happened, or even what *didn't* happen. All of it was necessary and all of it is to be appreciated. Because it has added to your value.

Try reciting this simple affirmation when you're in need of a little strength to embrace who and what you are:

I am fearfully and wonderfully made.

There is no part of my past that has permission to keep me from my future.

There is no person, dead or alive, who has the power to make me devalue my truth. I am who I am because of my journey and I love every bit of it.

Nobody can be me better than me and I love the steps that I've been blessed to take.

I'm prosperous, I'm blessed, I'm healed, and I am whole!

CHAPTER THREE

THE MIRROR EXPERIENCE

LOOKING AT YOU AND LOVING WHAT YOU SEE

There was once a fairytale that prompted the question, "Mirror, mirror, on the wall – who's the fairest of them all?"

Unfortunately, this question was asked by an evil queen who wanted the mirror to lie to her and tell her that she was the fairest. But deep down inside, she was mean and rude and hateful and some part of her knew that about herself. Darkness surrounded her, no matter how much she tried to pretend that she was light. And while there may have been a small element of outer beauty, the inner queen was horrible. It showed in her actions and her speech. It showed in the way she treated others and how she thought. It revealed what was in her heart by her disregard for the feelings of others. Yet, she wanted to be told something nice – even if it was a lie. Further, the talking mirror was actually possessed by an enslaved person that the queen had cast a spell on. But as jacked up as that may sound, there are many people who would rather accept the lie that they are perfect rather than embrace their flaws and love themselves through their individual processes.

These people are caught in a lying comfort zone; they want to be good, but lie to themselves so they don't have to choose the behaviors that will allow them to be what they want to be. So while the queen asked that question and stayed in her comfort zone of self-delusion, some of us need to be bold and confront the person in the mirror with honesty. In this confrontation, we have to accept the answers we receive and stop demanding the answers that we want to make us feel better. Yes, we want the truth to be pretty and promising; however, we have to break down the walls of ugliness to get there.

When was the last time you looked in a mirror? I mean really took a nice long look – without enhancements (makeup, hair, jewelry, etc.), without attempting to fix that strand of hair that was out of place. As a matter of fact, do you like to look at yourself without those *extras*? Do you even know who you are without them? This isn't about getting dressed for a special event or getting dolled up for a special night on the town with someone. This is about bearing yourself, looking YOU in the eyes, and asking one question: *Who am I*?

Unfortunately, we're taught that we have to have all the answers and that we have to know the stuff we don't know. We're often led to believe that once we hit a certain age wisdom and a Do Better mentality will automatically appear and operate within us. However, we can never learn the lessons we need to learn or have the answers to certain questions until we *first* learn who we are as an individual person. How does that happen? By having a mirror experience.

First things first, a mirror experience won't always occur by you simply looking in a mirror. That's more of a metaphorical approach. While it does have validity in the process of working to know who you are, it's about more than seeing your physical reflection. While looking in a mirror, you *do* see yourself, but do you REALLY see YOU? Unfortunately, we don't always see beyond the outer shell of our bodies. We don't see past what the mirror shows us. Very rarely do we look into our soul to discern the intricacies of our spirit.

Here are a few things that you can do to have a genuine mirror experience with yourself. The ultimate goal is getting to the point where you love all of you, flaws and freckles, strands and scars, marks and misconceptions, tests and tears. You have to learn to love ALL of you!

First of all, you have to *mind your mind*! Yes, it's synonymous with minding your own business; but this step entails you paying attention to the thoughts you have about YOU! Normally, there is about a 3 - 5 second window where one has time to shift unproductive and contrary thoughts to conscious thought so you can challenge that negative self-talk. We literally have thousands of thoughts per day. The thoughts can come from subliminal entities or they can come from real life issues. They can come from a commercial or a song; they can even come from a relative or social media. It's just like a commercial or advertisement that is playing in your head during each break in focus. Have you ever watched a commercial for a restaurant that was having a special or introducing a new dish? The pictures were appetizing, the colors were eye catching, the price was attractive, and the location was just close enough. There you were, doing laundry; suddenly you have a taste for that food which was advertised! When you see that ad for a second time, before you know it, you're grabbing your keys and heading out the door to go grub!

THAT, my friend, is the power of advertisement on the subconscious mind. And in that same way, life has a way of "selling" thoughts and ideas and opinions to us. There are things we believe that we shouldn't believe. There are portions of our life that we rehearse and force ourselves to act a certain way because we won't stop replaying the commercial or the trailer for that old film. **And then what happens?** We find ourselves being convinced to see things that aren't there or believe things that aren't valid. We latch onto things that mean us no good or we embrace lies that become comfortable. THIS is why we have to *mind our mind*.

There's a popular saying that goes, "Your mind is a terrible thing to waste." So is energy! Can you imagine how much energy and time we've wasted by thinking wrongly? By believing lies and deceit? By talking ourselves out of growth and peace? We do it all the time and don't realize it. However, that can change if we consciously make an effort to cast out anything that strips us of what we need in order to live in peace and joy. This is why the Bible tells us to "cast down imaginations" (2nd Corinthians 10:5) because there is power in our thoughts.

When we learn to observe our thoughts, we have the ability to filter them properly. We can easily remove unhelpful ones and push power thoughts to the forefront. So, for instance, when you begin to believe that you can start that business or write that book, then get discouraged and start to think the opposite, IMMEDIATELY tell yourself that you CAN! Then repeat that to yourself until you believe it. You have to take over what comes into your mental realm and kick out any intruders – those thoughts that don't align with peace and prosperity, healing and hope. If it makes you *stop* loving you, reject it quickly!

Don't be afraid to confront the truth. Often times we feel and think things because of subliminal messages. But there are times when WE are in the way of our own tranquility. Yes, we have mastered the art of blaming others – and there are times when they are at fault. Yet when will we ever look at ourselves and confront the crooked actions or thinking that we indulge in? Will we ever accept the fact that we're on a rollercoaster ride because we secretly enjoy the thrill, even if it makes us sick? Will we ever recognize that the enemy could be the *inner-me*? Yes, that might be a hard pill to swallow. Yet, if the truth is qualified to make us free, we have to know which lie we've fallen in love with and then replace it.

Some cultures have been conditioned to hide feelings of inadequacy, to not be vulnerable. This causes one to put up a front and to pretend that all is well, when it's really not. Before they know it, they've accepted this silent rule but it's causing them to be frustrated and miserable.

If you do a similar thing with your feelings, it's causing you to be stressed and depressed. It's causing you to be insecure and nervous. You have the power to confront everything that doesn't bring value to your life. YES, YOU HAVE THAT RIGHT!!!!! You don't have to accept things the way they've been; it doesn't matter how long they've been that way. YOU have the power to control it all . . . But it will cost you.

It'll cost you your old mindset and it'll cost you unforgiveness. You have to be willing to let go of those things when you decide to look in the mirror and confront the truth. You just may find out that you're more responsible for your happiness than anyone else.

Next, remind yourself of the many reasons you have to be grateful. Gratitude always has a way of putting things into proper perspective. Even if you have to literally write a list down, do that! When you're struggling with loving yourself or even liking yourself, write down the many things in your life that you are blessed to have.

Remind yourself of the instances where favor and grace were extended to you. Remember the times that you were sick, then healing met you. Remember the moments where life could have been taken, then grace covered you. Remind yourself of the times when you thought you were being rejected, then later discovered it was divine protection.

Focus on things that cause you to appreciate, rather than depreciate. Hone in on one of those elements that force you to realize you are sincerely and truly blessed. Discover the many ways that you have been allowed to live through what others didn't make it out of alive. Then, allow gratefulness to flood your heart and mind and emotions.

A fourth step to take while working on this self-reflecting step is to practice compassion – with YOU! When we beat ourselves up repeatedly, it causes us to stop seeing the good that lies within our souls. We replace our beauty with beatings, and wonder why we're internally covered in bruises. It's because we have danced with deceit for so long that our insides begin to resemble it. Before you know it, we become a pretty lie – which at the core isn't very pretty at all.

It's perfectly ok to tell yourself good things about yourself. You can be proud of your accomplishments without being prideful. You can be encouraging without being excessive. You can spoil yourself without splurging to the point of gluttony. If you spurge every once in a while it's ok! You have to have balance, have control; this is going back to the step about making decisions and choosing to make good decisions.

Pursue your passions by believing that you are good enough to live past the pain of your past! Recognize that you have the power to love every part of you – mind, body, soul – if you could just accept that you are you! You may see another person who appears to have it all together, be ok with *not* having it all together; just realize you actually know if that person really does have it all together. By now you know that we rarely get to see the whole person. In addition, be proud of the fact that you're progressing and learning to bathe yourself in positivity. And please, don't hold mistakes against yourself – even when you made them intentionally.

Every moment of our life is a necessary moment to shape us into the human beings we're called to be. Every bit of fire and every bit of rain, every major mess up and every ball dropping moment – all of it is working for you. It's all equipping you. It's all designed to unleash a strong you into the world. And you never know, there could be a multitude of people who are waiting to love themselves and waiting to appreciate what they see in the mirror — YOU could be thier example to show them how it is possible. Yes, your mistakes have the power to make you a mirror experience expert. The question is whether or not you will release your inhibitions and embrace your destiny. Will you?

At the end of the day, it's all up to you to love you and embrace you – good, bad, ugly or indifferent.

Love the parts of your story that make you cry as much as you love portions that make you laugh. Gain peace from the tornadoes, just as you do from the rainbows. Every part of who and what you are deserves to be admired. There is no way that you can build a house on an unstable foundation. So even when the beating and hammering and stepping on were occurring, it had to happen so that the floor could hold the walls and the ceiling.

Your healing will take place quicker when you realize that you first need that healing, but also when you will accept the choices that lead to healing.

There's nothing worse than having a gift that you refuse to open. So choose ye, this day, if you will love who you are or not. Choose ye, this day, if you'll receive healing or not. Choose ye, this exact moment, if you'll continue living in doubt and despair *or* if you'll see that you are worth having peace and love in your life. Nobody can force you to love the person you see in the mirror. It would certainly make life much easier *if* you could decide to. Please know that your past does not disqualify you from love. It doesn't matter how unlovable a past act or thought might have been, you can be free today. You can look in the mirror and have not one complaint today. You can enjoy every scar and every blemish, every follicle and every tear. Why? Because they're yours. And you are beautiful – the healed you is more attractive than you know. Make a decision to get to know *that* person!

Here is an affirmation for you that can help you during your mirror experience:

Today, I choose to release anything that keeps me from loving the me that I see.

I refuse to live in fear and doubt.
I refuse to accept the past as my present.

I will accept that my life is a blessing. The good and the bad have all made me who I am today.

At this moment, I wish to trade NOTHING for my journey. I am purposed. I am blessed. I am loved. But most importantly, I love me because God made me to be me.

CHAPTER FOUR

TRUSTED TO BE ACCOUNTABLE

TAKING PART IN YOUR OWN PROCESS

Accountability can be a tricky thing – then again, not so much. If you look up the definition of *accountable*, here is what you may find:

> subject to providing an explanation, give a report, or to justify something; to give an answer for.

Clearly, someone who is accountable has no issue with answering questions and giving a report. But the truth is that many people have an "I'm grown" mentality – often at the wrong time. People can be *grown* when it comes to relationships and money, they can be grown when it comes to paying bills or wardrobe choices; but when it comes to progress and process, they think they're too grown to have to answer to anyone. This is why many people get stuck and stagnant during their journey.

They want to be helped, but don't want to be given instructions on how to receive the assistance. They want the answers, but want them handed to them on a silver platter. And that is certainly *not* how any of this works!

Anyone who strives for success and growth must also embrace the various levels of accountability. But being accountable is not about having a babysitter. It's not so much about having someone to "parent" you and make sure you're doing right. It is, however, about helping you to eliminate those unnecessary elements in life that distract you and put you in a backwards motion. It's about teaching you to value yourself, your time, your talent, and your treasures. It's about making sure that you appreciate where you're going, without getting stuck in thoughts of where you've been. The key thing to remember here is that accountability is YOUR responsibility!

I know, I know – you thought it was about someone giving you the tools *and* creating the blueprint *and* walking out the process for you. On the contrary, it's more about you recognizing that you need to report your progress to someone who will remind you why you *must* stay in the process. It's about having someone who respects you enough to tell you when you're wrong and usher you towards being right. And yes, an accountability partner has the right to ask you questions and to check you when they see you going slightly astray. But you have to be willing to check yourself – and often! Does this mean that you're to be stepped on and treated horribly if you fail? Absolutely not!

It does mean that if you do mess up, two things are vital: your *resuscitation* and your *resurrection*. And when you have the right accountability measures in place, these two steps can catapult you beyond new mistakes.

What exactly do these two tools consist of?

Resuscitation is merely the act of reviving someone or something. It puts a degree of life back into something that was dead or unconscious. It causes movement and proof of life to reappear.

Resurrection is a word that is often heard in reference to Jesus. But it also indicates a powerful truth: you can get up from anything! By technical definition, it means *the state of being risen from the dead.* It denotes not only being resuscitated, but also getting up and showing that revival has occurred. And that is exactly what happens, or should happen, when one is accountable in a process where mistakes or accidents transpire. Because the truth is that we ALL mess up.

We won't always dot every I and cross every T perfectly. However, we have to be ok with going back and admitting that we missed some things. In admitting the mistakes, we make a conscious decision to not *live in* the mistake. And unless you can be trusted to be accountable, you'll find yourself always feeling ashamed for what happened or what you forgot to do or what you did wrong.

That's a horrible spirit called condemnation that tries to overtake us all. This is why one must be careful to constantly repeat Romans 8:1 in their spirit: *"There is therefore now no condemnation to them which are in Christ Jesus, who walk not after the flesh, but after the Spirit."*

When you are striving to walk in the right spirit, you'll trust the complexities of your journey – even when you don't like them and don't agree with them. But the act of being accountable will admit that, "I don't like it, but I'll trust it." Someone who is not accountable will say, "I don't have to do this because I'm grown!" And if you're not careful, you'll find yourself busy being grown and unproductive, unfulfilled, and unfruitful. When you think about it that way, that's not really being grown at all. If anything, that's a sign of major immaturity. However, healing and restoration can still occur at any stage that you find yourself in. As long as you're alive and well, you have an opportunity to take an active part in your healing. You have the ability to control your actions and your thoughts. You have to be willing to answer to yourself *and* to someone who is a little stronger than you are. That's perfectly ok!

Accountability isn't just a mindset; it's a *skill set*! Unfortunately, you can't list it on your resume but it is very much as important as the degrees and experience that you do have listed on a resume. Accountability shows that you have no issues with responding to those in an authoritative position. It proves that you don't mind being corrected when you're wrong and that you can receive direction when you're astray. It's not about highlighting your accidents as much as it's about highlighting your incidents. And while that word is often attached to something bad happening, it merely means *an individual occurrence or event*. It also means *something that occurs casually in connection with something else*.

What incidents have occurred in your life that bring you closer to where you need to be? What events have taken place that help push you towards a specific goal? These are the types of things you must learn to be accountable to – especially if you want to be restored and want to learn how to thrive with your scars. Your scars should never stop you from reporting to your success. Your scars should never keep you from being healed. Yes, there are people with scars and wounds and bloodspots that are still accountable to healing. Why? Because they know that healing is available; therefore, they report to it and remind it of where they are.

How can you be accountable? What can you do to learn this art?

First, you've GOT to tell the truth! Be honest about where you are and where you've been. Don't allow the lies that you've once believed to keep you from living the truth that you desire. Truly, it doesn't matter how unattractive the lie might be, there is a more beautiful YOU – scars and all – awaiting to emerge the moment you embrace truth. But you have to be willing to tell the truth. Be willing to tattle on yourself. In all honesty, we know we can be lazy and crazy at times. We know we are pitiful and prideful sometimes. We know when we're inattentive and uninterested.

That goes for all of us, so there is no reason to lie; we all fall short of our goals at different times in our lives. Yet, we still want to get better without having anyone *in our business*. And that is a major issue all by itself, which brings up the next thing we have to do.

Let someone *in your business*! We can be some of the most secretive people on the face of this earth, but at the wrong times! While there are things you need to keep private at times, there are also moments when you need to be able to confide in someone. And it has to be someone who won't pacify you in your foolishness. It has to be someone who loves you enough to pull you from in front of the 18-wheeler that's headed your way. This means you have to learn to trust *somebody*. Everyone is not your enemy and not everyone has a personal vendetta against you.

There are more people for you than against you, but they can't help you *become* you if you won't allow them to be who they're supposed to be *for* you! It's synonymous to going into the hospital. If you're checking into the emergency room and get called back to triage, you have to be willing to tell the nurse the truth about your condition. You mustn't leave out any details so that they can relay the information accurately to the doctor assigned to assist you. But if you show up to the ER saying, "I'm hurt, but I ain't telling you what's wrong with me," they can't help you. And you've just wasted valuable time that could have been spent in spearheading your restorative process.

So seek wise counsel, and then trust it. Maybe it's a relative or friend, maybe a co-worker or a neighbor. There are times when that person you can be accountable to and with is a stranger, who then turns into a confidant. Either way, any way a good accountability partner shows up -- embrace their assignment in your growth.

Thirdly, set goals and create a schedule to achieve them. This doesn't mean that you can control time – God's timing is what will ultimately win out. But when you have a plan, it helps Him (and others) to see that you are genuinely taking an active role in your personal process towards healing and freedom. In fact, Habakkuk 2:2 says, *"...write the vision, and make it plain upon tables, that he may run that readeth it."* What does this mean? Well, first of all, you have to write it out. There's something about actually getting a pen or pencil and a piece of paper and actually writing things down – in your handwriting. Yes, technology is great and helps us make notes quickly. Memorable moments occur and stick with our memory longer when it's just you and your handwriting. You feel what you're writing and you're birthing it on paper so that it can be birthed in reality. Our biblical advice doesn't stop there; that passage then says someone will read it and run with it. If you think about this, that's another level of accountability. Someone will read your vision (your goals and schedule). You've placed it out in the open to be critiqued. Then their mind can run with ways or resources to help you accomplish your goals. But you have to be willing to let them help you – not take over, not change and add their plan within, but genuinely help you stay on schedule and give you some general alarm clock reminders that will help you stay on task.

Another vital step to take as part of your process is that you have to ask questions.

There is such a wealth of knowledge available, but it often goes unused or hidden. Why? Because some people won't really seek it or ask the necessary questions to obtain it. Don't close off because of guilt, shame, shyness or any other reason. We have to dig deeper and find out why we choose to not know some things. Granted, you can't ask questions about what you have NO idea about. However, there are times when your brain becomes enlightened and inquisitive. There are times when you see something or feel something and want to know more. There are times you realize you have no clue about what you should ask, but there are always people around you to ask: church people of any level, a friendly neighbor, a teacher – anyone that seems to your heart there to help – go ask them for some guidance.

That's when you should write it down or take advantage of the opportunities to ask. Just in case you were told this lie as a kid, or maybe even as an adult – I want you to know that it's perfectly ok to inquire! You don't have to know everything, but you should take advantage of any opportunity to educate yourself. You should never let pride, your past or frustrations get in the way. The truth is that none of us know everything; but if we ask, we can learn anything.

These are just a few foundational steps that can help you. You must remember that accountability is for your benefit. It's to strengthen you, equip you and even heal you. Never look at it as something bothersome or as an imposition on another; you know that if you stop to think about people love to help others by sharing what they know. This goes double for an accountability partner who will be delighted to help.

The last thing you want is to walk around like everything is ok, but secretly struggle – at the hands of your own disobedience. You surely don't want to look at yourself in the mirror each day, question yourself about your progress, then not let anyone accurately assess you and give you pointers to mature. Nobody wants to deal with their ugly truths, but it's necessary. You have to be ok with accepting when you mess up or when you fall. We all fall. In fact, Romans 3:23 clearly tells us that we ALL have sinned and we ALL fall short of God's glory. But isn't it amazing that He doesn't give up on us and doesn't condemn us? Therefore, with that same understanding, we have to stop allowing false weights and secret condemnations to keep us in a place of bitterness and non-growth. The key is that you have to be willing to tell somebody you need help, and then respond to their genuine efforts to help you and bring clarity to your life.

We will never know it all. We will never have all the answers. But when we have people in our corner that can cheer for us *and* check us, we're more victorious than we realize.

Repeat this if you want to be more consistent with your accountability:

I am in complete control over the decisions that I make.

Today I am deciding that I need help. Getting help doesn't make me weak, it makes me wise and strong.

I will seek out the right person or persons to help push me to another level. Even when it gets hard, I won't rebut against the blessing of help that I receive.

I'm accountable and I'm accelerating because of it!

CHAPTER FIVE

JUST ASK

REJECTING PRIDE AND ACCEPTING ASSISTANCE

We touched on this a little in the last chapter, but this needed an entire chapter of its own. Why? Because pride has kept a lot of people from doing something as simple as asking a question. The late great actress Ruby Dee was once quoted saying, "The greatest gift is not being afraid to question." Believe it or not, countless people leave that gift wrapped, allowing it to expire before they open it.

Asking questions is a part of life. Every single second of every single day, life revolves around questions and answers. How else can you learn to differentiate the good from the bad? How will you know which elevator to take for your meeting or which road to take when traveling? How do you know what's going on with that doctor's report if you don't ask?

Let's take it back to childhood days. How did you get an answer as to whether or not you could go to the dance? The movies? A football game? How did you find out if that last cookie was up for grabs? The answer to all of those questions is simple – you had to ask! So when it comes to your healing and your survival, why are you afraid to ask for help? Why are you afraid to ask the necessary questions that can set you up for victory? I'll tell you why – because most people don't like to be in a position where they look needy or ill prepared. And while that's not usually the case at all, someone has led you to believe the lie that you will come off this way if you ask questions.

If you're hungry, would you rather starve or ask for food? And before you blurt the answer out to that question, genuinely think about it. Would you purposely sit around, stomach growling, head hurting, body weak, all because you're afraid or ashamed to ask for food? The ironic and unfortunate truth is that many of us sit at the buffet, see the food and smell the ingredients, but refuse to ask for a plate. And that's because we've allowed a weighty sense of pride to muzzle us. Yet it goes so much deeper than that.

You see, as children we weren't afraid to ask for anything – even if the answer wasn't seemingly in our favor. We'd beg and bug our parents or grandparents for that thing we wanted. We'd pressure siblings and cousins until they gave us the answer we wanted. Some of us would even ask teachers for answers to problems that they were teaching us to solve. In our innocence and foolishness, we didn't mind asking. Somewhere along the line we took "adulthood" to another meaning and decided that it was no longer feasible to ask for help.

That has been the dampening divide in our growth. How? Because we constantly *stunt* our growth when we don't retrieve the answers that can give us growth. All it takes is opening our mouths, but we won't do it. So we're left with voids that could have easily been filled. Beyond this, we set ourselves up for filling up with and on the wrong entities.

If you go to a gas station and there is an Out of Order sign on the pump you pull up to, you don't get mad and leave the entire store. Instead, you look around and mentally ask yourself if the next one is open. You put the car in drive and go around until you find a pump that is active. Nowadays, you can pay at the pump. But years ago, you would have to go in and ask a question like: *May I get $10 on pump nine?* You'd hand the cashier your money, possibly get a receipt, and go back out to pump your gas. I want you to pay attention to something. Did the cashier get upset that you asked them a question? No! Did they deny you the right to pump after you paid? No!

So after we've suffered and endured all that we have, after we've paid our dues (in time and suffering), why are we afraid to ask for refilling? Why do we have an issue with seeking help to be healed? And who told us that we're "ok" in not asking?

Two of the greatest misconceptions in the world when it comes to *just asking* are these: *asking questions makes you weak* and *you should already know*. These 2 ill-stated soliloquies have confused people all over the world. And they come from faulty seeds that were planted by someone else who didn't understand the power in asking questions.

Asking questions can literally be a life or death situation. When you ask the right questions, you can save a life or kill something before it kills you. You can open up doors to a wealth of knowledge or close doors that were created to trap you. But you have to ask the necessary questions first. If you want to grow, if you want to heal, if you want to thrive *with* your scars, you have to ask the right questions.

Don't be afraid of sounding crazy either. That's something that often comes to mind and keeps us quiet. There's a saying that goes, "The only dumb question is an unasked one." No matter what question you have, there is always a response for it. Yes, there may be times when you don't want or don't like the answers you were given. Nevertheless, there was still an answer. You will never know unless you ask, right? Right!

The truth you have to know and accept is that no matter what … you DO NOT have to do *it* alone. You can put whatever you'd like in that "it" spot; the fact remains that you sincerely don't have to feel like you're the only one going through the process or that you're the only one who has ever had to feel what you're feeling. On the contrary, Ecclesiastes 1:9 explains to us that there is nothing new under the sun. So that very thing you've dealt with, or are even currently dealing with, has happened to someone else at some point in their life. If you have ever read anything in the Bible, you'll see the same things happening today that happened then – just in different time or eras.

A wise man is known for asking questions to gain clarity.

When you ask questions, you also have to know who to ask. There are instances where we have stop asking questions because we've been asking the wrong ones and getting the wrong information. One of the greatest aggravations and disappointments in life is depending on someone to help you that simply couldn't do it. Maybe it was intentional, but most times there was a genuine attempt made to give you the assistance you needed. But somewhere along the line, the ball was dropped. Just when you thought a winning score was on the way, defeat showed up on the court or field. This left a bad taste in your mouth. It made you feel that you should've never asked this person and that you personally failed. But sometimes, the other person simply isn't qualified to answer us. Sometimes, the person we're asking just can't or just doesn't know how to help us. We have to be ok with that. It might even be someone you love dearly. Yes, it can be someone that you expect to have the answers you need. The truth is that there are some people who will claim to help you, because their heart is in the right place, but their limited resources and knowledge simply won't allow it to be so.

Another hard pill to swallow is that we often won't ask for help because we don't want to change. That's right, some of us have become infatuated with our crutches and forgot that the crutch was supposed to be temporary. Some of us have fallen in love with leisure leadership when we're called to operate at a legendary leadership level.

We don't want the change because we don't want the responsibilities that come along with it. It's much easier to blame others for our inability to get help when we don't really intend on asking for it because we've become comfortable right where we are. The truth is that some questions we ask will cause us to lose some bad habits. It'll cause us to let go of excuses and delays. If we learn to ask the right questions, we may become candidates for thriving with our scars – but unfortunately, many want to just be seen with the scars and want to receive the sympathy, but don't intend on getting better. Because in getting better, we might lose attention. Remember the step about looking in the mirror and being truthful with yourself?

There is also a myth that if we ask questions, we'll immediately be judged. The consensus statement of this era we are living in now is "don't judge me." We allow a lot of answers to float in the atmosphere looking for a home in the midst of a society more concerned about offending you than maturing you. Yes, this is very real! We don't want it to appear that our lifestyle and decisions are under a microscope. So we hide the little knowledge we do have in hopes of it not exposing the ugly truth that we're lost and need directions. Struggling in silence has become a badge of honor when it should be banned if you honor your destiny and your healing. Pride and presumptions should never overtake your ability to get up from the pit and proceed towards prosperity.

We also don't like to ask questions because technology and social media have made us anti-social. We've become so dependent on virtual relationships and emoji conversations that we panic at the first sight of having to actually speak to someone and get more information from them. We don't value friendships as much because online besties come a dollar per dozen. So we dare not ask anyone for anything; because when there is a need, we'll just type it vaguely and see which "follower" will respond. This is still not the way of truth, not the way to take to become a better you. So how do we fix it? What do we do to make ourselves comfortable with asking for help and receiving it?

First, you have to stop beating around the bush. You don't have to make your question sound comfortable for the hearer and you don't need to prolong the scenario around the question. Just ask! If you need a Band-aid or directions, just ask!

Second, don't feel obligated to help them in return. Just because you ask someone for help or guidance, that does not mean that you'll be in the hot seat the next time they need something. While there's nothing wrong with wanting to be there for them, you might not be the one who can help them in the same way they help you. That is completely ok.

Third, stop assuming that others don't want to help you or that they're too busy. You don't know their schedules, their resources, their knowledge nor their abilities to see you through. Assuming they don't want to help you or have something better to do is not proper. If they're showing that they want to help, let them help until they show you otherwise.

There's nothing wrong with swallowing your pride and accepting the assistance that's assigned to you. When you feel otherwise, repeat this affirmation:

Help is available to me and I am going after it.

I will not talk myself out of the resources that are available to me and I refuse to sit in fear or condemnation.

I will ask, I will seek, and I will knock. Because in doing that, the door will open for me.

CHAPTER SIX

GOOD COMPANY

SURROUNDING YOURSELF WITH THE RIGHT PEOPLE

The Brooklyn based Hip Hop group, *Whodini*, hit us in the 1980s with a song that still poses relevancy today. In their chart topper, *Friends*, they asked, "Friends, how many of us have them? Friends, ones we can depend on?" While so many were boppin' their heads to the beat, there were some who actually stopped to think about the song's message. Yes, some actually started to consider their circle of friends. And this made many evaluate the connections that they had with those they had deemed as being a buddy, a confidant, a bro or sis, a friend.

What exactly is a friend?

By definition, a friend is *a person whom one knows and has a mutual bond of affection, typically exclusive of sexual relations.* When polled, others have stated that a friend is someone they trust, honor, respect, and even protect. But every now and then, we all need to stop and do two things concerning the friends connected to us: *take inventory* and *do an appraisal.*

When you take inventory of something, you basically check for numbers. This is to see the quality and quantity of what you have in stock. When the numbers don't add up, you take note and make a change.

When there's an appraisal, this is inclusive of determining the value of something. You make an honest effort to judge the nature and quality of a thing. While there are no price tags on people and genuine relationships, there should be appraisals done to ensure that value is being added to your life instead of depreciation taking place. Just like with jewelry, you need to see if your connections are worth being insured. And when they are not, this can lead you down a dangerous road of humps and bumps — especially if you're not in good company.

When you're in good company, people who will lift you and love you will always surround you. You're connected to those who will enhance you and encourage you. Being in good company also means that they won't steer you wrong and won't allow you to steer yourself wrong. To the contrary, being in the midst of people who love *and* like you is vital for your healing and growth. It is certainly not about being around a cloud of witnesses that always appease your flesh. No, good company is not a group of people who say yes all the time, a group that will agree with you all the time and only say things to flatter you.

Instead, good company will challenge you to be better and celebrate small victories just as vibrantly as they'll celebrate large victories. If your company isn't diverse and doesn't offer a pool of wisdom, you're drowning yourself in complacency and defeat already.

You want friends who are strong, but different, to help strengthen you. In fact, there is a scripture in Proverbs 27:17 that tells us *iron sharpens iron*. Two strong entities are rubbing against each other, in order to sharpen both. Imagine iron rubbing up against iron. You're sure to see sparks fly and pieces falling off. You may feel heat and might even get a little burnt. The final result is you in your full power!

Please don't choose popularity over peculiarity. Making the decision to go with the crowd can lead you down a path that you're not ready for. Choosing iron challenges you to heighten your senses and intelligence. If you can't learn or grow with those in your circle, you're actually in a cage. It makes no sense to be bound and stuck with people who are supposed to go and grow with you but only hold you back. It's dangerous and poisonous.

There's nothing worse than being in horrible relationships or connected to poisonous people who you're trying to live a full life with. In that atmosphere, you will always find yourself tired and irritated. You'll always be frustrated and probably confused. There will always be tension and turmoil. Why? Because your inability to work together will make the road much longer. The drama and the gossip, the inconsistencies and the ill will; they're all guaranteed to be a stumbling block if you let it. That's why an inventory check and an appraisal are necessary.

You've sometimes got to calculate the value being brought. Even check to see if you are bringing value. Good company isn't just about them, it's also about you! Do you have negative conversations with them? Are you the one who brings others down with the way you talk or think? Are you surrounded by people who fit the saying that "misery loves company?"

These are valid questions and points you need to consider. It's very true that the sum of one's success lies within the top five people they surround themselves with. Who is in your circle? And what are you all talking about and doing together?

1 Corinthians 15:33 tells us, "Be not deceived: evil communications corrupt good manners." You have to ask yourself what you and your friends talk about and make sure that it's conducive to where you're headed, not contradictory to your goals and dreams.

Recollect some of your dialogues. In doing so, you just might find out who it's time to disconnect from; even if that person is you! If the things your friends talk about make you feel weird and icky once you're out of their presence, they just might not be the good company you thought they were. That's ok.

Seasons don't last forever, and neither do all friendships. Some are designed to teach you specific lessons and some are designed to push you through to a better place. A more mature place. A happier place. Those in your circle should want you to succeed and live a healthy life. If they're always bringing drama your way or always trying to talk you out of wisdom you have, RUN!

A little love from the right people can make life so much easier. Even when you have to be corrected, you will know their heart and will undoubtedly see that their iron personality is only trying to sharpen you because it wants you to be prepared for the battles ahead. So the message to you is simple – make sure that your good company is not good to your flesh, but good for your spirit.

Ensure that it's good for your emotions and mental stability. Be very sure that prayer and encouragement and chastening take place in this circle. You surely don't need the opposite when you're pressing forward and working at thriving. Your scar is a reminder of where you've been, but it's your company that should help you not live in the place of the scar's inception. Those scars should help you to see the progress and remember the valuable lessons learned, but they should no longer be the path guiding your mind's focus.

Here is another way of looking at it: when you have a specific type of cell phone, it takes a specific charger to refill its energy. The device can't be plugged into just anything and not every charger is qualified to restore its power. The same thing goes with your circle of friends. Not every person that you meet has the capacity to handle you when you need recharging. And that's ok! It doesn't mean that anything is wrong with them. They're just not *for* you. So be ok with not connecting with everyone.

Also, be ok with excusing yourself from anyone that's carnal or shallow. Dismiss those from your life who are going nowhere fast and who get upset if it looks like you're not going with them. That is the time to run. You should never feel obligated to stay somewhere *just* for the sake of staying. When there is high energy, laughter, respect, and accountability – you've got a good circle of friends.

What about those times when you have to be your own good company?

Do you *like* you?

Are you comfortable with hanging out alone? Can you look yourself in the mirror and love what you see; flaws and all? Proper connections are necessary; you have to take a step back sometimes and reconnect with YOU.

Everybody needs alone time *sometimes*! Taking a moment to revisit our thoughts, taking a moment to journal our feelings, embracing a few seconds of fresh air with no one around us – all of these are examples of partaking in good company with yourself. At the end of the day, it makes no sense to be surrounded by a crowd and still feel alone!

Try this affirmation to remind you of the importance of good company:

Today, I choose to surround myself with the right people.

I won't allow my past to limit me to the love and light that I need and deserve.

I don't need to fit in, I need to stand out. And I will because my process matters.

Only positive connections are welcomed in my life, and I am the first partaker of that rule.

I am love, I am light, I am good company.

I am connected to sources that charge me properly.

CHAPTER SEVEN

FORGIVENESS MATTERS

LETTING GO OF THE GRUDGE

Take a moment to inhale . . . now exhale.

Yes, you needed to breathe deeply in order to dive into this next step. As you already know, this book is about helping you thrive with the scars you have. Let's be honest, some of you reading this haven't been able to thrive because you've not forgiven the things or people that were the origins of your scars.

The scars that you have are indicative of something happening, whether it was your fault or not. Depending on how deep the wound is, the thought of how you received each scar can be very touchy. It can have you feeling emotions and thinking things that you didn't want to feel or think. It can have you doubting yourself or even other people.

Today, you need to know this: as much as getting the scar may have hurt you, you have to forgive the situation and the people so that healing can really emerge.

What exactly does it mean to forgive?

By definition, forgiveness means *to grant pardon of an offense or a debt*. It also means *to cease feelings of resentment against*. There are many facets to the act of forgiveness. One thing remains true about it; it's necessary for growth and healing! However, it has very little to do with the other person. Yes, forgiveness is to benefit you and to stabilize your emotional and mental health, even your physical health.

The act of forgiveness accomplishes so many goals, with the first being reducing anger. Certainly we all get angry – sometimes at others and sometimes at ourselves. *Unhealthy* anger is extremely dangerous, especially when not dealt with. When ignored, it becomes cancerous and deadly. Your thoughts and your entire being can be tampered with when you are holding onto unhealthy anger. Please understand, it's ok to *be* angry. What you do with that anger is the real issue. And when it causes you to act out of character or keep you bound in any form, it has just become your god and your puppet master. You have to ask the question of *who* or *what* is controlling your responses?

The Bible tells us in Ephesians 4:26 to "be ye angry, and sin not: let not the sun go down upon your wrath." This simply means that you have the right to be angry, but don't let anger become who you are and how you operate. You have to deal with those issues and memories that have brought that feeling of anger or disappointment upon you.

You have to address those things that hurt a little so you can heal a lot.

Forgiveness comes when you recognize why you're hurt, why you're disappointed, why you're frustrated . . . then make a decision to move forward and enjoy your life.

The act of forgiveness also gives you room to grow. We often utter prayers or wishes to become a better person and to learn how *not* to let things get to us. But what we fail to realize is that we have to be tested in the areas of our prayers so that WE can see if we really want what we ask for.

For example, those who pray for patience have to be mindful of asking for such a trait. Because what will happen are instances where your patience is tried and you'll feel pushed to the limit. You'll endure times where things that get on your nerves will be allowed to get on your nerves. How will you know you got the answer to your prayer – patience – if you then are never put in a situation which requires that patience?

So in this same manner of thought, if you've ever prayed for a heart that forgives, you will be tested in a magnitude of ways that require you to have to forgive. And while we stated earlier that forgiveness is more for you, it still comes in 2 forms:

> *forgiveness of others*
> and
> *forgiveness of self*

When you forgive someone else, you're declaring that you acknowledge what they did *but* you'll not let it control nor consume your thoughts. You're saying that the pain was real, the disappointment was real, the deceit was even real, but that your peace means more than holding a grudge. From there, you learn what category to put these people in.

Does forgiveness of others mean you have to be their best friend and constantly put yourself in predicaments to be around them? No, not at all. It does mean that you get to decide how long their offense will offend you. You see, every decision that you make in this process of forgiving others is totally based upon you.

This puts you in the driver's seat and ensures that no one holds anything over your head – as long as YOU don't allow it! Even beyond this, when you choose to walk in unforgiveness, you stand in the way of your own progress or forgiveness with God. Matthew 6:14-15 talks about the importance of forgiveness and how it opens the door for us to be forgiven. In essence having the ability to forgive is good. It relieves us from carrying false burdens and being stuck in yesteryear. However, true forgiveness occurs when you forgive yourself.

Let's be honest – maybe it was your fault and maybe it wasn't. Maybe it could have been prevented and maybe it could not have. Maybe you should have known better and maybe you thought you did. At the end of the day, you cannot allow the enemy to play with your mind and hold a spirit of condemnation over you. You cannot allow these negative thoughts to take up residency in your life. Because when you do, you make it almost impossible for forward movement to take place. You have to forgive YOU if you want YOU to grow and heal and thrive.

Please understand that you're not the first or the only person who has ever done something wrong. We all make mistakes; and truth be told, sometimes we like it in the moment. Regardless of the who, what, why, when, or any other question that may come along for each mistake – extending mercy is acceptable, even to yourself. When you choose not to forgive, you invite a cloud of darkness to overshadow everything that you attempt to do. You invoke negative vibes and beat yourself up unnecessarily. But in this moment, freedom is yours!

As you read these words and take deep breaths, forgiveness is becoming more and more *doable*. Forgiveness for them and for you is just as realistic as the breaths you're breathing right now. And this is why you have to forgive.

You must forgive because negative energy doesn't have to keep you bound. You deserve more. You must forgive because you are worthy of compassion and peace. You must forgive because you deserve to feel love in an unconditional manner. You must forgive them and yourself because you're missing out on valuable lessons and limiting your influence if you stay locked up in guilt and anger.

You have the right to forgive your parents, your ex, and even that friend who betrayed you. You must forgive that sibling, that stranger, and even that pastor for what was said and done. Forgive them for what they said, whether it was the truth or a lie. Forgive them for not taking up for you, even if they promised they would. Forgive them for making you believe in them, especially when their intentions were never pure. Forgive, forgive, forgive.

Where do you see yourself in the future? Do you see yourself free and prosperous? Do you see yourself in a position to help others move forward? Or do you see yourself as a puppet?

While the last question may sound a bit twisted, we should never let anyone or anything negatively manipulate us and try to coerce us into anxiety and defeat. Unfortunately, that is exactly what unforgiveness does. It makes us a puppet to depression and despair. But we have the ability to cut the strings and be the author of our own next chapter. We can cease and erase every ounce of judgment and self-sabotage by one simple act of forgiveness.

Thriving with your scars is not about ignoring them, but appreciating their place in your life and forgiving their intrusion while embracing their lessons. Forgiveness *is* the key that unlocks doors of positive patterns and progressive pushes. So forgive – them and yourself.

If you need a little help reminding yourself why you should forgive, repeat this affirmation:

I forgive everybody I've ever encountered, even myself.

Every perceived wrong will now receive my light and love.

I am accompanied with understanding, peace, strength, and healing. For that reason, forgiveness is easy to me. Because all things worked, and are working, for my good. So my scars don't scare me and my past doesn't haunt me.

I am delivered, I am whole, and I am forgiven.

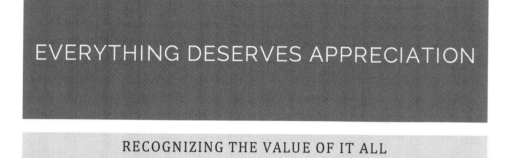

CHAPTER EIGHT

EVERYTHING DESERVES APPRECIATION

RECOGNIZING THE VALUE OF IT ALL

How is it possible to be grateful or thankful for bad things that happen to good people? What value does pain have to any process? The best way to answer that question is to think about childbirth.

During childbirth, it is said that a woman comes the closest to death that she will ever be. But in most cases, that's not at the forefront of a mother's thoughts. She goes through moments of weight gain and cravings, her body is stretched and made uncomfortable, she even deals with medical issues and having to accept that her body is no longer her own. And it doesn't get any easier from there.

Afterwards, she goes through labor pains and breathing exercises. She is forced to make a decision on how to bring the child safely through a natural birth or choose the opening of her stomach. Her body grows, twists, and turns as she prepares for the arrival of her baby – growing closer and closer to death.

After all of the stretch marks and pushing, after all the inhaling and exhaling, what happens? A new life is delivered into the world. And suddenly, nothing bad that occurred is even considered. Nothing painful takes precedence. Instead, gratefulness and excitement take over the heart and emotions. Those feelings come because the joy of a baby has permeated the room and every portion of the birthing process is appreciated.

Good things can be appreciated fully when bad things occur in the interim. Otherwise, how else could you appreciate sunshine and rainbows unless you've experienced rain? As much as you may hate what was done to you, it had to happen so that another side of you could be revealed. Yes, the scars are real. No, you didn't ask for them. But if you stop and think for just a moment, there are some extremely valuable lessons that you learned ONLY because of certain incidents that happened.

How else would you know that you could win a battle — unless you've been in a fight? What would be the indicator that your heart is healed if it has never been broken? Would you be able to measure stormy days if you were never forced to walk in the rain? Every single scenario given so far points back at you doing one thing: learning to appreciate everything!

There's a scripture in 1 Thessalonians 5:18 that reads, "In every thing give thanks: for this is the Will of God in Christ Jesus concerning you." *Everything*? So that means even the things you didn't (or still don't) agree with?

Yep! ALL of it! Note that the ending of that verse is extremely weighty. How can even the *bad* stuff that caused scars be the Will of God for one's life? How can a God who is loving and merciful allow pain to come one's way and still call it good. Well, here's an explanation.

In the book of Job, we are told a story of a man who did absolutely nothing wrong. He was considered faithful and was a true man of God. But one day, the devil was granted permission to mess with Job's life. If you've never read this story in the Bible, please do. It's very interesting. Yes, Job lost 99% of what he had – from children to land, animals to possessions, even lost his good health. But it was all ordained and allowed. And in the end, he gained back so much more than what he had. He was healed, his family was restored, and his faith in God proved him to be notable. But during the process, it was undoubtedly hard for him to deal with the physical and mental discomfort of it all. However, it was all necessary.

It was ALL necessary.

Because Job trusted God, he was able to appreciate the fact that God believed in him enough to be trusted with this trial.

Did you know that the very thing you're haunted by was actually entrusted to you? It may seem a bit crazy and may sound unrealistic, but there are things that you have faced – and are even facing now – that have been entrusted to you. It's hard to see the good when everything hurts so badly. It's hard to appreciate the lesson when the pain is prevalent. It is extremely hard to see the scar as beautiful when it hurt so badly to get cut so deeply. But if they had never cut you, would you know that you could still lead while you're bleeding? Would you even know that survival *in* that situation was possible? If your flesh was never punctured, how would you recognize healing when it showed up? This is exactly why every step in every process of our lives is necessary. For me personally, I had to learn this through failed relationships and making decisions that would ultimately paint me in a negative light.

As a teen or a young adult, we feel unstoppable. We always believe that tomorrow will come and that no matter what we endure, everything will be ok. In fact, we don't often think of the detriment that we could possibly cause. We just live, do, experience, and see what happens. We made decisions with little to no information. And usually, it's because we want to prove a point or we simply want to be rebellious. For me, I had my spurts with just that. Yes, I was intelligent. Yes, I was independent. But back then, I would have looked at you crazily if you would've told me that I'd be married more than once. No, I would have never accepted that I would have lost a child. You certainly couldn't have told me that I would have spent time in jail. But the irony in it all is that it was ordained for me to suffer so that someone else wouldn't have to.

Being a single mother was never part of my personal plan; however, God promised that He would be faithful. And even in the highs and lows of single parenthood, He has been just that. Now, have I always felt *good* about it? Absolutely not! Have I learned to accept it? Definitely. Because I now know that every detail, good and bad, was beautiful in His eyes. Every test and trial, every setback and heartbreak, every loss and tear – all of it is now in a place of appreciation because I recognize that it was necessary.

You might be in a place right now that's extremely uncomfortable. You may have experienced some events that you don't think are or were purposed. But none of it has caught God by surprise. While we were shocked by what happened and while we wanted to deny the very reasons that it happened, it happened with purpose. And even when the enemy wants you to believe that you're suffering for nothing, you have to know that he is evil and his insinuations are lies. For this reason, the lesson of "weighing" is vital.

Even when we can't see it, everything in life has a scale. Each scale depicts the weight that something holds. Yes, some things are heavier than others. But that doesn't diminish value on the lighter things. It just means that some things have the propensity to carry more and to handle more. And while we don't see ourselves this way, we are more weighty emotionally and spiritually and psychologically than we realize.

Why? Because God knew what we would need to accomplish whatever He has ahead of us. He was, and is still, well aware of everything attached to us and its purpose.

Some things are made to strengthen us and some things are made to break the wrong things off of us.

At the end of the day, it ALL has value. And it is ALL crucial for our growth and healing and elevation. Learning to appreciate the events that led to the scars we have will enable us to recognize the importance of the scars themselves. And yes, it's ok to look down at the scars or to think about the hurt that was once there and say, "Thank you!"

Never be afraid to see the beauty and value in the unattractive things that made you stronger and wiser. Each element merits admiration.

Each time your past tries to negatively remind you of what you've endured, combat that energy by substituting it with appreciation.

I am not ashamed of my scars because they beautify my destiny.

I decree and declare that every part of my process was and is vital.

In order to heal, I must embrace the hurt and appreciate that I was chosen to endure it.

My scars matter, just as much as my healing. And my tests matter, just as much as my testimony.

Everything in my life has value and I appreciate my process.

CHAPTER NINE

THIS MOMENT IS EVERYTHING

LIVING IN THE NOW

If any lesson has been taught in this new age, it's that we need to capture the moment. Society will spend time taking selfies and updating posts. People of all ages will document an event, just to prove that they were there. But if you ask someone to share with you the details and the emotions they experienced, they'll most likely pull out their phone. And that's because not many people live in the NOW.

They live in the documentation of it, but honestly have no idea how it really makes them feel. This leads to having memories that are just hanging in space, waiting to be claimed, but left to fizzle. This is why you have to learn to live in the NOW! With everything that happens, no matter what it is, you need to experience the array of emotions and thoughts that occur while you're actually in it. And if you're on a road to healing, it obviously makes sense to know how it feels to be healed vs. simply knowing that you are healed. While the ending is a blessing, the beginning and the middle are just as important. We have to live in that moment, as it's happening, and gravitate to all that it injects within us. But what exactly does it mean to live in the *now*?

Living in the *now* is all about awareness. It means that you're completely focused on, and centered on, the here and now. It means that you're not worrying about anything in the past and you're not concerning yourself with what's to come; but instead, you're breathing in every moment of the life that is happening right now — in the present moment. And yes, there is a time to recollect and project. But sometimes, we have to focus on the present moment. And that often means without the enhancements of technology, or even other people!

Being present in the *right now* can actually lead to better health and happiness. You won't have to worry about anxiety, because thinking about the What Ifs of the future will make you nervous. You won't have to worry or be tormented by rumination 2-steps and dancing with stress. You won't have to *picture* a horrible ending or a fearful beginning.

You simply need to breathe and be grateful for where you are right now. Yes, there are always things going on that could attempt to steal your attention. Sometimes, you have to be ok with being selfish and only indulging in the present moment. However, I agree, that can be difficult to do.

We are always encouraged to think ahead and plan for the future, which definitely has its time and place. We even consider how busy we are and all that we're tasked to do, which also holds a level of importance. That's why we have to learn to balance those things. We can't let the future consume us to the point that we're not cognizant of anything else.

Mastering this will, however, take some major balancing. During your balancing acts, you have to make sure that you're not carrying around unnecessary weights. There is a scripture in Hebrews 12:1 that tell us to "...lay aside every weight, *and* the sin which doth so easily beset us..." This is clearly indicative that there are some things we carry, while trying to live in multiple moments at one time, that cause us to push ourselves out of the Will of God. So in the midst of all that you're carrying and in the midst of you *saying* that you're living in the moment, you have to make sure that you're not carrying sin and extra weights. You have to ensure that everything about your walk, about your process, is in line with God's Will for your life and that it's not pulling you away from Him.

There's also another scripture that tells us to cast all of our cares on Him, because He cares for us (1st Peter 5:7). Most times, we don't know how to cast our cares on Him and live in the individual breaths that He gives us because we're too concerned with how to spend the next one. We have everything on our minds, except for the right thing.

Then what happens is that we have spent so much energy on what *will* happen that we miss what *is* happening.

This causes us to be anxious and nervous and moody and a plethora of other emotions – none of which can help us where we are nor catapult us to where we need to go. So we have to learn the art of gratefulness in the present moment.

We have to learn how to experience the experiences of the now. Because the truth is that it's *now* or *never*! If we don't live in the now, right now, we'll regret the chances that we missed to experience the life that was waiting for us. We'll regret the chances we had to embrace the healing and peace that was afforded us, but we missed them because we were scattered in thought and spirit. And it'll be nobody's fault but our own. But if we can't focus and appreciate life, we'll never appreciate the now.

We talked about appreciating the value of everything in our life. Because where we came from is very important. But we can never focus so much on where we came from that we don't realize where we are. We can't get stuck on how it happened and diminish the value in the fact of it actually happening. We have to practice being here – wherever *here* is at the time we're in it.

The one reason that *this* moment is EVERYTHING is because it's causing you to be grateful for life. It's helping you to see that what was meant to kill you didn't take you out. Living in the now helps you see that all of *that* was necessary in order for you to know that you're alive and in place right now. Appreciating that peace, welcoming that joy, will create a less stressful life for you.

Great - how do you do it? How can one really have a healthy balance of planning, recollecting, and resting? Here are a few suggestions.

First, don't dwell on the past too much. It's perfectly ok to have small doses of memories to revisit. Maybe you're trying to trace your steps to see where you made a wrong turn or a wrong decision. Maybe you're just remembering something great that happened and mentally reliving how it made you feel. Don't stay there too long. Oftentimes, when we indulge in the past then we endanger progression for the present and future. Even in that time of memory, focus on the many ways that your present has benefitted from your past so that you are connecting your full life (past, present, future).

Another thing you can do to balance living in the moment is learn how to improve your ability to accept.

Accept what?

Accept all that has occurred in order to realize what's going on. Often times, we refuse to live in the now because we don't think we're ready to face what it's brought with it from the past. However, in acknowledging the past and being hopeful for the future, you still must savor the present and not lose track of it. Time is already uncontrollable so don't get in the habit of rushing through the present, thinking about everything else.

You can also learn how to enhance your engagement skills. When we engage in something, we take our focus off of idleness and often even off of self. This will also kill the notion of being comfortable with being an introvert. While this is an issue for many people, it has also become a stumbling block for many. They minimize engagement opportunities by saying that they're too afraid or too tire or uninterested. Some will even go as far as saying they don't want the "drama" that comes with mingling and engaging.

We have to realize that not *all* company is bad company. And not all engagement is bad. But in some regards, social media has crippled us and allowed us to only engage with someone through a fictitious page or behind a fake name. That's a dangerous place to be in because it depletes us of opportunities to network and actually live in the now with other people. It is also dangerous because we know it is a false reality, one where people put on their best face in a best case situation and lie at worst. Don't engage with deception.

Another way to have a healthy balance of living in the now is to let go of your clutter. Oftentimes, we hold on to possessions and thoughts and many other things that take precedence over that which is really important. It's synonymous to being a hoarder. By definition, a hoarder is someone who accumulates stuff while believing that it will be necessary for future use. That does have its place and time, but there are those who go slightly (or greatly) overboard with what they hold on to. And for someone who is trying to heal and progress, even with the reminders of their hurt, you have to learn when to let go of that which isn't beneficial to your progress.

There's a saying that goes, "If it doesn't add to you then it subtracts from you. And that's the wrong side of the equation to be on." This is vital to remember with everything in life. If it subtracts from you or divides your emotions and focus, you have to really check its purpose in your life. Because balance means that everything is spread evenly and equally, with necessary purpose. Anything otherwise is in the way and usually very harmful. Don't get into the habit of holding onto things or people or memories, just because you might need it or them later.

It's just like clothing in a closet. If you're holding onto things you've not worn in years, chances are that you're not going to wear them. So let them go!

The ultimate goal is always to thrive and heal and progress and manifest. You can't live in the future until you live in the now. You can't appreciate the future if you have no idea what's happening in this moment. You'll never get all that you can *then* if you don't see the value in what you have *now*. Be ok with taking a breather.

Embrace letting go of all the stuff that floats in your mind about yesteryear – even if just for a moment. Give yourself a chance to be better by sitting still for a moment and realizing that you deserve to be better.

Healing can come in so many forms and so many ways, but you have to sometimes breathe and let go of what's making you sick so that you can heal. And that takes place when you look at where you are right now and appreciate the simplicity of the immediate moments you're given. Tell yourself:

I am deserving of the greatness in my future, but I also appreciate my present.

Every second that I am given, even now, is pivotal and I appreciate it as much as the next.

This breath right now is vital, this view right now is vital, this emotion right now is vital, and my decisions right now are vital.

I am successful in my future because I am living in and appreciating my now!

CHAPTER TEN

TAKE THE LIMITS OFF

DENOUNCING FEAR OF THE UNKNOWN

Everything that was created has a purpose, yet there are various areas in life where boundaries are to be welcomed. If you have a 2-story home and a toddler learning to walk, a safety gate is advisable to keep the child from hurting themselves on the stairs. If there's a bridge out a couple miles ahead of you and you start to see large signs blocking the roadway -- that is definitely something to protect you. Even as it pertains to germs and illnesses, there are people who walk around with a mask over their nose and mouth – this prevents their germs from exposing their cold to others and vice versa. All of these represent instances where boundaries are permissible.

But in life, there are times when we put boundaries and limitations where they should not be. Inadvertently, we keep ourselves from moving. We keep ourselves from thriving. We keep ourselves from living the life that we were designed to live.

That's a dangerous thing to do.

By definition, a *limit* is something that declares confinement of another thing. It means that there is a cut-off to a specific area or person that is marked as the furthest distance permissible. While everyone has their reasons for embracing limitations, there are times when limits can hinder us and cripple us. One of the most dangerous canals that lead to limitations is that limitation called Fear.

There's an acronymical approach to the word *fear* that states it's meaning is:

F *alse*
E *vidence*
A *ppearing*
R *eal*

This signifies that someone who lives in fear will only go to a certain point in their life – be it relationships, business, ministry, education, etc.

Our minds are a force to be reckoned with, yet we often don't realize the true power there. We seldom accept and adopt the mindset that we can do anything we put our mind to. Yes, we recite it. Yes, we get excited about it in the moment The unfortunate reality is that many of us miss out on some powerful life events because we've allowed fear to create barriers. We've allowed fake scenarios to make us believe that one thing will happen over another, usually something negative. We allow past failures and bad decisions to make us believe that a mistake is all we're worth creating. So we live in trepidation, often expecting the unhealthiest circumstances to become our truth.

All the while we forfeit gifts with our name on the box, believing that it'll never work out for our good. That's usually because we've gotten so interdependent on disappointment that we don't think we deserve its opposite. We seem to do this even though something new and fresh and exhilarating awaits us – all on the other side of fear – but we don't go after it.

As it pertains to love and relationships, there are countless people who have missed out on genuine happiness all because of fear. They set limitations on possibilities, for various reasons. Some followed traditional family trends while others went with what their parents said. Some refused to cross color lines while others grappled with a 10-year age difference. There are even those who refused to give love another try because of failed relationships or simply emotional damage that was caused by previous ones – thus, creating borders and blocking out all of the good that was available to them. Thus, we have people who miss out on love because they don't believe it'll ever be good to them or for them. This is usually because their mindset was wrong about love in the first place.

Another way we limit ourselves, allowing fear to hold us hostage, is when it pertains to our destiny. There are many people who are called and assigned to do certain things – things that go beyond ministry. The word "called" is often coupled with a church title; realize that assignments are bigger than that. Yet, there are some amazing people with influential gifts who refuse to function in them because of wayward thinking.

Someone won't start a business because they don't have a degree. Someone won't write a book because they're not personally the greatest speller. Someone refuses to serve on a committee because they don't want to step on anyone's toes whose been in place longer. And then there's someone like me – someone who receives a call of pastoring, but initially refuses to walk in it because they think they are not worthy.

It was on Resurrection Sunday of 1999 when my pastor made an announcement in church. He was providing a list of books that every leader needed to add to their library, mainly for ministry, and I began writing those book titles down. My mind was nowhere near focusing on doing anything in a ministerial capacity. However, I felt it could assist me in my political endeavors. Suddenly, he asked each person that wrote the books down to come to the altar. Immediately, I got up and walked toward the front of the sanctuary, crying my eyes out. It was then that I heard the voice of God telling me He *did* call me to serve the people, but not as an elected official right then – but in ministry.

I remember saying, "I am NOT called to pastor, so I don't know what You're going to do God!"

This was in no way shape or form on my To Do list for my life. I enjoyed serving in other capacities and I loved to assist people. But to stand behind a pulpit, to be a senior leader over a flock of people – no way! That was NOT my plan nor my passion. Yet, it was God's purpose for my life.

And it didn't matter what fears or apprehensions I had about it.

It didn't matter what horror stories I'd heard about leaders or even the chaos that I may have witnessed through my past pastors. God called me and He was *not* going to accept any boundaries put up to keep out His Word for my life.

Needless to say, I did my initial sermon in 2000 and was appointed as a pastor in 2018. I tried to run, I tried to hide, I tried to reject it. But when God has made a decision about it, no barriers that we put up can stop Him.

I had to be willing to let go of all the noise and aggravation that tried to take precedence over His Plan. I had to let go and let God have His way, on a major level. Because if I were to deny Him access, there's no telling how my life would have turned out. And I don't think I want to know.

When you have the strength to denounce fear, you grow muscles that you didn't know existed. You gain confidence that was seemingly never there. You reach heights that once appeared to be too far away. And you usually shock yourself, thankful that you took a chance on yourself.

Yes, that's exactly what happens when you tell fear that it is *a liar*. Instantly, the acronym for *fear* takes on a different approach and becomes:

> **F** ace
> **E** verything
> **A** nd
> **R** ise

You make a decision to silence apprehension and anxiety. You make a decision to kick down the doors that keep you stuck and complacent. You make a decision to let the mind of a winner cancel out the mind of a whiner.

When you decide to face everything and rise, you are telling yourself that no circumstance has permission to keep you in bondage any longer. You become a change agent and seek out opportunities to better yourself, while not being afraid of the *what ifs* that present themselves to you. In life, there are always pros and cons. Just because the cons are real doesn't mean they have control over the outcome. When you're set to take the limits off of yourself, you open yourself up to all positive outcomes that are looking for you.

You welcome success, you welcome happiness, you welcome prosperity, you welcome love, you welcome second chances, you welcome forgiveness, you welcome new connections, and you even welcome a better and stronger YOU! How do you get to that place? How can you denounce fear and stop bottling up your possibilities?

First, you have to control your thoughts. Scripture tells us, in 2nd Corinthians 10:5, that we have to "cast down imaginations and every high thing that exalts itself against the knowledge of God..."

This implies that rancid and tainted thoughts will creep in. Just as sure as night is the opposite of day, there will always be something negative that tries to overpower something positive. Even in that knowledge, we have to learn how to cast the negative down and out. We have to denounce it and call it powerless. We have to take its authority and use it to kill the stinking thinking. Yes, WE have to do it ourselves.

If it doesn't edify you and bring you closer to your destiny, you have to be careful in how you entertain it. While still being grateful for it showing up, so that you can properly identify it, is a valuable outlook; you must still know (decide/choose) what is to be danced with and what is to be left aside. So if it deplores your success and your purpose, you have to condemn it quickly – without hesitation!

Next, try journaling. Often times, we allow our imaginations to run rampant. And in most cases, it's running in the wrong direction. Control your thoughts by controlling your narrative. Begin journaling the best possible scenarios that you can imagine. Even when fear tries to intercept and take over your focus, ignore it by writing down its opposite and elaborating on it.

For example, if you have a fear of heights and don't want to travel by airplane, write in your journal how you would imagine the most perfect flight to be to your most desired location. Maybe you want to visit an island or an ancient city in Europe. Perhaps your heart is in the continent of Africa or your taste buds long to visit an Asian land. Wherever you want to go, write a story in your journal of what your ideal trip would be like *if* you weren't afraid of heights. Before you know it, you'll be creating the most beautiful and most realistic story of how you're traveling the world – in the very thing that you *think* you fear. If you write the vision and make it plain (Habakkuk 2:2), you never know what will come of it and how it will work out for you!

Another healthy activity that you can do is learning how to channel your doubts. Instead of allowing them to be a means of you getting stuck and confined, use them as motivation and fuel. Each time doubt comes, laugh at it and declare that it's powerless. Anytime you get pushed back into your comfort zone and become unsure whether or not you should jump, do it anyway! JUMP! Push back and get back out there. There's absolutely nothing wrong with getting pushed to the edge because that is often where you find yourself. The question is this: are you really ready to encounter the *other* you that has been dying to live?

Doubts will often make you dig deeper and ask hard questions. So instead of letting the doubts put up stumbling blocks, use those doubts to build the bridge you need to cross over to faith. Push past the normal responses of doubt and inhibitions and kick your way through that wall to reach a happier and healed *you*!

Something else you can do is celebrate the small victories and still plan for larger goals. Oftentimes, we place limits on our small goals and only strive to attain these small goals. We have to conquer the small ones, while still striving to meet and surpass the greater ones! Bit by bit, this causes us to move bricks that we've used to put up walls. And we all know that when walls are up, it's hard to see what's on the other side. On the other hand, when you celebrate small victories and prepare for greater ones, you permit yourself to remove the bricks that keep you sequestered. So celebrate moving one brick now while planning to move 2 or 3 the next time. Before you know it, you'll encounter an entirely different life that fear was trying to seclude you from all along.

One of the greatest gifts that you can give yourself is that of positivity.

If you see a hurdle, believe that you can jump it – and then do it! If you see a fence, believe that you can tear it down – and then do it! If you encounter a mountain, believe that you can climb it – and then do it!

There is nothing that has the true ability to stop you *but* you. And you have to make up in your mind that you are worth living past the limitations that you and others have set for you. Sure, there are healthy boundaries that everyone must have. That's not what we're referring to here. You have to deject and denounce every boundary that stunts your growth and depletes you of your peace.

This affirmation can help you do just that:

I have the power to create happy and healthy boundaries in my life. Those boundaries keep me safe and keep me in a place of prosperity.

Fear does not reside in my boundaries. Only success and love are welcome here, because I am loved and I am successful.

I am not afraid of the unknown, I anticipate the day that I can encounter the unknown – because it knows me and awaits my arrival. Therefore, my past has no power over my present.

I forgive myself for opportunities I've missed due to fear. Now I am no longer it's slave. I am healed, I am whole, I am thriving, and am taking the limits off. Because I can be and do whatever I desire – and I WILL!

CHAPTER ELEVEN

USE YOUR WORDS PROPERLY

SPEAKING SUCCESS BEFORE YOU SEE IT

Many of us have heard scriptures like Proverbs 18:21, that tells us death and life are in the power of the tongue. We've heard Psalm 19:14, that bids an earnest request for the words we speak to be acceptable in the sight of God. We've even recited, with all seriousness, how the words we speak will have to be given an account for, Matthew 12:36. Yet, that is one of the greatest habits that we lack discipline in – using our words properly. If we truly believed that we could create our atmosphere with our spoken words, we might take more care into what we put out there. Yet, we talk too much and speak our minds quickly — wondering why things don't seem to be getting better. If we replayed our conversations into our own hearing, we might be shocked by how we've limited our forward movement and ourselves merely by what we allow to come from our mouth.

Scripture also tells us that out of the abundance of the heart, the mouth speaks (Luke 6:45). So does that mean that when we speak damnation or doubt, that's what lies within our hearts? Does that mean we gravitate to negativity and spew it with every other word, that our heart is also cancerous and poisonous? Apparently so!

We have to be aware of the weapon that we have with our words, especially when we're in a process of healing and elevation. It can be difficult to thrive with scars if you're constantly referring to your scars as something horrid and pointless.

If you never see the appreciation in the process, as we learned before, you'll never be able to complete the process the way it was intended. And if your mind and heart focus constantly on the negative things, that is what will essentially come from your mouth.

The words that you speak and the dialect that you lean towards become the house that you build for yourself. Therefore, if you don't like where you're living then you need to recreate your space. You need to shape your environment and your "living arrangements" by restructuring your vocabulary and your beliefs. After all, even your thriving depends on what you say — yes, with the scars that you have.

First of all, hold yourself in a position of power. This doesn't mean to become condescending or arrogant. This doesn't mean to start looking at *yourself* as being above everyone else. This does mean, however, that you must walk and talk as though you *know* your words mean something. You have to place value on what you allow to come through your lips to the ears of others, even your own ears. Your entire countenance should resemble that of someone who humbly recognizes who they are, flaws and all; and that they are a worthy and wise human with gifts to share.

Your body language and your words should indicate that mediocrity has no place in forward advancements. You have to know what you're saying, all while meaning the words that you release. Those words have to add life and hope, while killing despair at the same time. It's not about knowing every word in the dictionary and thesaurus. It has nothing to do with what college degree you have or what socioeconomic category you fit into. It IS all about knowing your value and your position.

Secondly, you have to express yourself in a way that evokes positive change. Learn to cancel out "I can't" and "I don't know" phrases with "I can" and "I will learn" statements.

This is the art of reframing and shifting. Earlier, we said that what you say is synonymous to building your house. So if you've been using the wrong foundation or the wrong brick and mortar, reframe and shift. Replace the verbiage that your old self is used to using and add affirmative words instead. Never feel the need to express what you cannot do. While there are things that you may not know how to do yet, always speak that you *will* learn or that you *will* do whatever goes in that blank.

For example, if you continue to say, "I can't cook well," then you'll never be able to cook well. But you can replace that with, "I'm going to learn how to cook better," then you're shifting the negative towards a positive and reframing any doubtful outcomes.

Next, be careful in how you label yourself — inwardly *and* outwardly. While we may see it as *keepin' it real* or *tellin' our truth*, we often paint ourselves in such a bad light that we eliminate the possibility for illumination to occur through us.

Labels are a subconscious mental boundary that places us in position to always belittle ourselves, and accept when others do it to us. This is why many of us can't thrive with our scars because we've allowed our scars to be a bad thing instead of a propelling thing.

We have the right and the authority to change the narrative of the labels stamped on us. For example, if we say that we are "lazy" and that we hate being such, we promote the agenda of our laziness. Therefore, we don't put the expectation on ourselves to respect time or deal with it wisely. We don't set goals with realistic effort because we've already internally decided what we are and are not going to complete as it concerns most of our tasks. We reinforce the behaviors of that label instead of stripping it of its power.

Here is another example. We can be given opportunities to meet others and some of us may immediately say, "I'm an introvert. I don't *do* people." And while that is a very valid condition for some, we have to recognize that it has a lot to do with the mind. Now, I'm no medical doctor and my place is not to diagnose you, however the complaints of an extreme introvert and the behaviors of one, usually stem from a traumatic experience that has made them feel uncomfortable around people. They find it hard to trust others. Unfortunately, this limits the reach of healing. Because in order to heal properly, you have to encounter something or someone that resembles what hurt you. You often times will have to go through the same test, or a similar one, to see if you've healed from the first test. You can't *be* human and not want to deal with the human population. Yes, some people can make you feel that all us humans are *crazy*. You'll never know what happens until you step out. You just have to stop labeling yourself because this limits you.

Another way to speak success and use your words properly is identifying problems as opportunities. Everyone has a problem or an issue that they have to encounter. We all deal with life instances that we most likely would rather not deal with; it's a part of life. Every single human has to learn to deal with these events. However, what you speak determines how you see a thing and vice versa.

If you see the problem as an opportunity, you'll not crumble and panic. If you see an issue as an instance for growth, you'll take the blows a little better. Think of it as a rainstorm. While the rain may cancel your plans for a picnic or the entire parade, it will also provide nourishment for crops. It washes away dirt and filth. It revives and cleanses. So while the picnic was planned and while you desired to lie out in the sun, you can know the rain was necessary so that you can appreciate the sun all the more. Pouting over the rainfall and throwing a tantrum will not fix anything. In fact, it will ruin the moods of those around you as well as your own mood. Learning to smile in the rain and be hopeful for the rainbow is what it's all about.

You can also look at it this way . . . I remember a relationship that I was in. This gentleman swept me off of my feet. We had a great time together, laughed and traveled together, made amazing memories together. However, there was one problem – he refused to match me spiritually. He loved family, he loved experiencing life, but he did not enjoy going to church and was not into that lifestyle. For me, that was all I knew. It was what I had become accustomed to. It was my foundation. My relationship with God was number one in my life. No matter how many times I had messed up, God was always there. However, I had to make a decision one day. And it was difficult. I loved this man and I wanted to be with him. But my pull for living for God was greater than my attraction and need for him. So there came a time when I had to obey God and my instincts. And this was a definite learning experience for me.

Yes, I could have doubled down in despair due to my track record with relationships. But I had to see the lesson in this. It was an opportunity for me to prove to God that I loved Him more. It was a chance for me to show my spirit man that my flesh was not in control. And although it wasn't easy, it was worth it.

Maybe a relationship isn't your issue. Maybe you struggle with looking at punishment *as* punishment.

We know that to everything there is a season, a time and purpose under the heavens. Ecclesiastes teaches us that.

Another moment of turning a problem into an opportunity was when I found myself stuck in a jail cell with the current wife of someone from my past. I was already embarrassed, being a local government employee and being arrested on DUI charges. This was not supposed to be happening to me. My boss had to be called immediately, so that was a fear of mine — losing my job, that is. Then I was assigned inside this particular cell during my first weekend of five that I was ordered to complete and *she* was there.

Now, from the outside looking in, one would assume that I'd buckle under pressure and embarrassment. One would assume that I'd be snooty and disrespectful towards her because of how our pasts intersected. To the contrary, this was a God-orchestrated moment. It became an opportunity for healing to occur. She and I talked and mended and bonded in a way that was unexpected. We used the power of our words to bring about healing and restoration to a situation that could have gone another way.

For that opportunity, I am forever grateful. It showed maturity and the power of understanding. You see, we were both dealing with the same issue. Little did we know that The Father would use our mistakes to glorify Him and make a liar out of the real enemy. Any opportunity to prove the enemy wrong is a chance worth taking.

Once again, this proves what can happen by using the proper words. We talked and shared and understood one another on a totally different level than I expected. It was a shock to see her there, for a moment my heart bounced off the ground and my spirit started to sink; but I'm so glad that we had the conversation; it was necessary.

Words can make or break us. They can heal or harm. They can strengthen us or tear us down. It's those private conversations that we have with ourselves that really matter.

When you find yourself needing a little direction in speaking properly, use this affirmation as a guide:

I am confident and powerful. I know my words create my world and the words I speak will only create peace and prosperity.

My words create healing and wholeness. My words are a form of love and not hate. They turn trials into triumphs and make every moment memorable. I know what to say, I know how to say it, and if I don't have the right words to say – I'll stop, breathe, think, and regroup my thoughts. Because only words that build up are allowed to come from my lips.

Every word that I utter speaks God's stamp of approval over my life. I am thriving with my language and it is no longer a barrier.

CHAPTER TWELVE

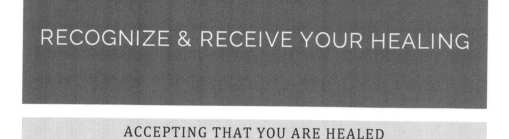

RECOGNIZE & RECEIVE YOUR HEALING

ACCEPTING THAT YOU ARE HEALED

We can be so cognizant of the weather and the world around us, but we often can't see tiny changes within us that prove one thing: *we are healed*! Matthew 16 starts out by telling us the dangers in being able to discern the weather, but lacking the ability to discern the signs of the times. In this same manner, there is no valid reason why we should know more about what's going on in the world than we do with our own bodies and minds and emotions.

You went through a horrible ordeal. The pain was real, the scars are real, the memory is real. Still, have you noticed this fact: *you survived what you thought would kill you?!*

Did you even take time to realize that you are truly a warrior? On top of that, have you noticed that it doesn't hurt like it used to? More times than not, we fail to see the positive changes and the growth because we've grown accustomed to the noise and the chaos. We've embraced the bleeding and the bandages. If we'd take a moment to remove the bandages, we just might see that while there is a scar, we are healed.

A scar, by definition, is a mark that is left by a *healed* wound, sore, or burn. It is any blemish that remains as a trace of an injury, now indicating that the injury is no longer an active wound. Think about that — we walk around, crying about our scars and praying for the pain to go away. We fail to realize that the scar is usually indicative that it doesn't really hurt anymore. The scar is a badge of honor given when a soldier has lived through a battle and made it to the other side of the war. Yes, scars are the first sign of healing. So why don't we like scars?

Most scars are usually unattractive in nature. They cause a darker or lighter marking on our skin, so it shows a flaw. Scars prove that something was once wrong or in pain. And we tend to try our best to remove the evidence of the pain, instead of looking at the blemish as proof of the promise that we made it out alive and alright. But who said scars were dreadful? What person made us believe that our war wounds are unpleasant and unwanted? The majority of the time, it's us!

WE are the ones who over think about our scars and try to find ways to hide them. It's time to stop and look at the fact that our scars prove we've made it out of some of the most tumultuous times of our lives. And that goes for the inward scars, as well. So, other than the appearance of a scar, how do you know when you're healed?

First, you're no longer afraid of the possibility of "it" happening again. Most times, if you endured it the first time then you know you're able to come out on top another time. No, you may not want to. But you never know what you can handle until you're forced to handle it. So taking "it" (or the idea of *it*) like a champ is a sign that you've healed.

Secondly, you don't live under the premise of what "they" say or what "they" think and feel. True healing comes when you're no longer concerned with the chatter; you're focused on moving to the next chapter. You make a choice to not be held captive by the past, nor those who played a part in it. Instead, you allow it to be just that – the past. And no matter who does or does not like it, you can genuinely smile and move forward.

Third, you love yourself enough to be honest. Sometimes, healing can't take place because we refuse to deal with the reality of a situation. Be it a relationship, something that happened as a child, corporate connections, or dealing with loss and grief — we have to be ok with accepting that these things happened. Once they occur, we can't pretend like they didn't. The scar didn't just put itself there and it's admirable to talk about it. Yes, you may cry the first time or two you deal with it. But healing takes place, and has taken place, when you can discuss the damage without diminishing its existence. Ultimately, it has pushed you towards your destiny. You have to confront it and deal with it, head on. When you're able to do so without fear and shame and inner turmoil, you know that healing is your portion and your prerogative.

Healing also shows that it has arrived when you can sleep well at night. Yes, something as simple as a good night's rest is indicative of peace coming in. And when you have peace, you can rest. When you can rest, you can wake up revived and ready to thrive. From childhood throughout adulthood, we're told of the importance of getting a good night's sleep. It does so much more for your psyche than you realize. Yes, it energizes the body and helps prepare you for a greater tomorrow. But it also equips you to think clearly and to be more apt to respond properly. Resting at night causes you to not ponder on the pain, it prepares you to be positioned for the promise of wholeness. And that's what we all what.

At the end of the day we all want to be whole and happy. We want to be healed and restored. We want to not look like what we've been through. That is very possible, but you have to recognize the portions of you that *are* better and not bitter. That's a sign of healing. You have to see that you're not the same person you were back then. That's a sign of healing. You have to pat yourself on the back for not crying today or yesterday. That's a sign of healing.

It's ok to be proud of yourself and recognize all the ways that you have matured. After all, you were trusted with those fights and your scars are to be worn with honor. Because just as God considered Job, He considered you for all that you've endured. Why? Because He could trust you. Don't ever doubt that you are healed. When life tries to make you relive the pain, repeat this:

I am not what happened to me and I am not ashamed of what happened to me.

In fact, my scars are beautiful and I'm grateful for them. I wear them with pride because they prove my longevity and my status as a warrior.

I am healed, and I know it. I am free, and I know it. I am whole, and I know it. I am a victor, and I know it.

My mind is healed, my body is healed, my emotions are healed, and my destiny is sealed – and I know it. Because God is within me, I have not ever failed and will not ever fail.

Healing is always my portion and I gladly embrace it, from the inside out.

CONCLUSION

In order to thrive with my scars, I must first accept that I am flawed and that I do have scars. However, they do not stop me from being successful and they don't disqualify me from greatness.

THEREFORE:

I make a conscious decision to grow and receive my growth, not as condescending but as propelling. Growth is necessary and I accept it.

I will walk in my truth and embrace every part of my journey. While there are parts that I didn't understand initially, I wholeheartedly love and appreciate everything that makes me ME.

I am no longer afraid to look in the mirror; I will embrace what I see and love what I see. I won't be ashamed of my reflection and will no longer hide from it. Instead, I will stare at it and see the beauty in what's revealed.

I also recognize that I need help on this journey. Therefore, I will not abuse or mistreat those who are assigned to push me into my destiny. I will honor and respect the art of accountability and will take an active role in my own healing and deliverance so that soaring is inevitable for me.

I will no longer allow pride to keep me from receiving what I need to succeed. I will use my resources and openly see what assistance awaits me. Everyone is not an enemy and I can no longer treat them as such.

I will surround myself with those who mean me well and want the best for me. I will no longer feel guilty about severing relationships that are toxic because I know that I deserve peace and people that love me.

I will not allow grudges to hold me hostage; instead, I will forgive and let total healing take place — mind, body, and soul. Forgiveness is my weapon of choice.

I will appreciate every step in my process and know that it was all necessary. Because even when it didn't feel good, it was working for my good. And I'm grateful.

I won't waste time living in the past and I'll not try to over think the future. Instead, I will thank God for this breath and this moment and this opportunity. Because as quickly as they come, they will go. So I must take advantage of the now RIGHT now.

I decree and declare that fear is a powerless liar and that I am no longer a slave to it. All limitations, roadblocks, and barriers have been revoked and none of it has permission to hold me hostage any more.

I am now in control of my words and I only speak that which edifies and strengthens me. Negative labels are detached from me immediately and only words of power and healing belong in my vocabulary.

I am healed,
I am restored,
I am favored, and
I am thriving.

I no longer see disgust in my scars; I see destiny in them.

Even with my scars, I am thriving. I am prosperous. I am rejuvenated. I am successful. I am whole. And I feel amazing.

ABOUT THE AUTHOR

REGINA CLAY

 Regina Clay is a mother, daughter, sister, and woman of God. Born in Baltimore, MD, and raised in Columbia, MD, she is the product of Mr. and Mrs. Jasper Clay, Jr. She accredits her relentless pursuit and relationship with God to her upbringing.

She was baptized at the age of 12 and willingly served in ministry throughout her years. In 1999, she answered the call to ministry and preached her initial sermon under Bishop Frank Madison Reid, III (Bethel A.M.E. Church) in 2000.

Her educational journey includes receiving a Bachelor of Arts degree in Communications in 1986 from the University of Virginia at Charlottesville and a Masters of Divinity from Howard University 2005. She's served with the State of Maryland in the Department of Human Resources and Human Services. She's also functioned as a Community Liaison with the Howard County Government. Regina's latest job assignment was as Howard County District Manager for Congressman Elijah E. Cummings. Later (2016), she founded the Regina Clay Consulting Group,

LLC. With vast experience in human services, relationship development, and research, she's right where she desires to be: in a position to help others.

She also serves in The Links, Inc on the Eastern Area Wellness Committee and locally in her Columbia, MD, Chapter as Parliamentarian. She's earned the respect and trust of several while aiding the Large Girl Scouts of Central Maryland on the Board of Directors. And recently, she's been appointed as the pastor of New Queen Esther A.M.E. Church.

Simply put, Regina Clay is a woman who is determined to *live full and die empty*! She recognizes that her existence is for an even greater purpose. And she gracefully welcomes everything that The Father entrusts her with. She lives by Philippians 1:6, but makes it personal by saying: "*I am confident in this very thing, that He which hath begun a good work in ME (Regina Clay) WILL perform it until the day of Jesus Christ!*"

From the pulpit to the marketplace and everywhere in between, Regina means business . . . KINGDOM business!

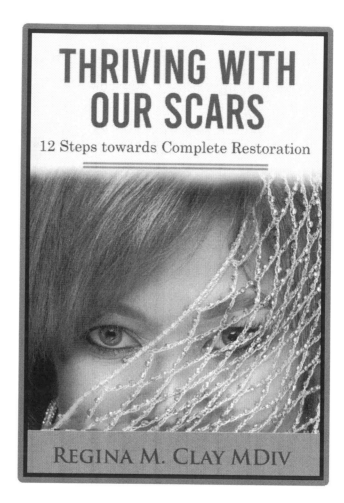

THRIVING WITH
OUR SCARS

12 Steps towards Complete Restoration

REGINA M. CLAY MDIV

Connect with Regina Clay online!

www.ReginaClay.com

facebook.com/ReginaMClay

@iamreginaclay

Made in the USA
Middletown, DE
28 March 2022

63256134R00073